Network Theory and *Nashville*

FILM THEORY IN PRACTICE

Series Editor: Ryan Engley

Editorial Board

Slavoj Žižek, University of Ljubljana, Slovenia
Joan Copjec, Brown University, USA
Hilary Neroni, University of Vermont, USA
Jennifer Friedlander, Pomona College, USA
Fabio Vighi, University of Cardiff, UK
Hugh Manon, Clark University, USA
Paul Eisenstein, Otterbein University, USA
Hyon Joo Yoo, University of Vermont, USA
Louis-Paul Willis, University of Quebec, Canada

Network Theory and *Nashville*

ZACHARY TAVLIN

BLOOMSBURY ACADEMIC
NEW YORK • LONDON • OXFORD • NEW DELHI • SYDNEY

BLOOMSBURY ACADEMIC

Bloomsbury Publishing Inc, 1359 Broadway, New York, NY 10018, USA
Bloomsbury Publishing Plc, 50 Bedford Square, London, WC1B 3DP, UK
Bloomsbury Publishing Ireland, 29 Earlsfort Terrace, Dublin 2, D02 AY28, Ireland

BLOOMSBURY, BLOOMSBURY ACADEMIC and the Diana logo are trademarks of
Bloomsbury Publishing Plc

First published in the United States of America 2026

Copyright © Zachary Tavlin, 2026

For legal purposes the Acknowledgments on p. ix constitute an extension of this
copyright page.

Series design by Alice Marwick
Cover images (from top): Abstract © gremlin / Getty Images; Publicity image from
Nashville, 1975 © Paramount Skydance Corporation

All rights reserved. No part of this publication may be: i) reproduced or transmitted in
any form, electronic or mechanical, including photocopying, recording or by means of
any information storage or retrieval system without prior permission in writing from
the publishers; or ii) used or reproduced in any way for the training, development
or operation of artificial intelligence (AI) technologies, including generative AI
technologies. The rights holders expressly reserve this publication from the text and
data mining exception as per Article 4(3) of the Digital Single Market Directive (EU)
2019/790.

Bloomsbury Publishing Inc does not have any control over, or responsibility for, any
third-party websites referred to or in this book. All internet addresses given in this
book were correct at the time of going to press. The author and publisher regret any
inconvenience caused if addresses have changed or sites have ceased to exist, but
can accept no responsibility for any such changes.

Library of Congress Cataloging-in-Publication Data
Names: Tavlin, Zachary, 1989- author
Title: Network theory and Nashville / Zachary Tavlin.
Description: New York: Bloomsbury Academic, 2026. | Series: Film theory in
practice | Includes bibliographical references and index.
Identifiers: LCCN 2025029030 | ISBN 9781501388217 hardback |
ISBN 9781501388200 paperback | ISBN 9781501388187 pdf |
ISBN 9781501388194 epub
Subjects: LCSH: Nashville (Motion picture) | Actor-network theory |
LCGFT: Film criticism
Classification: LCC PN1997.N332 T38 2026
LC record available at https://lccn.loc.gov/2025029030

ISBN: HB: 978-1-5013-8821-7
PB: 978-1-5013-8820-0
ePDF: 978-1-5013-8818-7
eBook: 978-1-5013-8819-4

Series: Film Theory in Practice

Typeset by Deanta Global Publishing Services, Chennai, India
Printed and bound in the United States of America

For product safety related questions contact productsafety@bloomsbury.com.

To find out more about our authors and books visit www.bloomsbury.com and sign up
for our newsletters.

For Preska: "Seen any good movies lately?"

CONTENTS

List of Figures viii
Acknowledgments ix

Introduction 1
1 What Are Networks? 17
2 What Is *Nashville*? 103
Conclusion 193

Further Reading 199
Index 202

FIGURES

1. Moretti's *Hamlet* Network. Reproduced with the permission of Franco Moretti 58
2. "Now, after years in the making . . ." All film stills are taken from *Nashville* 107
3. Walker invades the picture 119
4. Airport, curbside 125
5. L. A. Joan's arrival 133
6. Character gridlock 135
7. Studio A 147
8. Studio B 148
9. Linnea looks back 160
10. Sueleen at "the smoker" 161
11. The Grand Ole Opry, brought to you by Goo Goo 165
12. Kenny and his violin case 173
13. A backstage view 180
14. Barbara Jean, icon 183

ACKNOWLEDGMENTS

In the big network of characters supporting this little book, there are a few important hubs:

Anna Kornbluh was the first to recommend that I write something about network cinema for this series. Todd McGowan was still series editor at the time and encouraged the project from the start (and though he wished that I picked a different film, he never stood in *Nashville*'s way). Katie Gallof Houck at Bloomsbury oversaw the whole process with superior patience. Stephanie Grace-Petinos was there the entire way too, always making things easier for me to manage. Ryan Engley took over the series halfway down the line and gave this book the generous, supportive, and judicious editorial vision it needed. And Kirin Wachter-Grene, to whom I owe far more than I can say here, was the one whose existence made it possible for me to even finish the book when another part of me wanted to throw everything away, quit my job, and . . . I don't know, go work for the Standard Candy Company designing new Goo Goo Cluster flavors (something that, now that I'm saying it out loud, could be a thing someday—the ball is in my current employer's court).

Introduction

Network Elementals, Network Etymology

Network theory is more than a loose collection of theses about social, informational, and narrative relationships, but less than a clearly articulated program of social, informational, and narrative analysis. Network theory, we might say, is itself a network of theories, and not as codified as a tradition or as part of any single discipline. Network film theory, more specifically, is more than a scattered series of critical texts that examine the relational distribution of characters, objects, locations, and motifs in narrative films, but less than an identifiable school of thought with a stable set of classic works and authors to keep going back to for definition and a sense of mission.

This book aims to corral the sprawling plurality of theoretical approaches to networks by emphasizing the interpretive obstacles to and advantages of thinking in terms of network form. Network theory is a standpoint on the world that understands phenomena of all sorts to exist relationally in distributed, mesh-like forms. When narrowed to focus on narrative texts, including films, network theory traces the story mesh or net formed by the text's discourse as a primary step in the process of critical interpretation. Robert Altman's *Nashville* (1975), our lodestar, serves as an exemplary film both in the structural and stylistic demands it makes to be viewed as a network of connections, and in the difficulties it presents for our ability to map those connections with the cognitive tools we typically bring to the movies. One of the creative apexes of New Hollywood cinema, *Nashville* helped establish network form—with its plurality of crisscrossing, multi-directional plotlines; large character ensembles without central protagonists; and relatively wide but shallow story worlds—as a viable mode of storytelling on screen. Altman's film also continues to raise, as we continue to watch it, some of the same questions that pop up whenever we ponder the implications of our social world's ever-intensifying reticulation.

A network, defined technically but simply, is any structure made of nodes or vertices and links or edges. Nodes or vertices are points where two or more pathways intersect; links or edges are the pathways themselves, the channels that connect nodes. The size and complexity of a network depend on the number of nodes and the number of links between different nodes. The more links connecting a node to other nodes, the higher its degree. The level of connectivity within or across a network is a matter of degree, or average degree, between all its nodes. The more nodes a network has, the more links are required for that network to approach complete connectivity (the limit case being one where all nodes are connected to all others). And as the number of nodes increases, the number of links required for complete connectivity increases disproportionately, like in an exponential function. Not all nodes in a network necessarily share the same number of links. A network's distribution can be more or less balanced or symmetrical. Nodes with a large relative number of links to other nodes in the same network are called hubs, like the central part of a wheel from which its spokes radiate outward toward its periphery. In a visual diagram of a network, hubs will appear to center specific clusters of nodes, as if serving as regional capitals on a map of a larger nation.

If a network is to "work," connectivity is everything. Two recent books on networks in the arts and media begin with E. M. Forster's famous ventriloquism, words from the mouth of character Margaret Schlegel in his 1910 novel *Howards*

End: "Only connect!" I am referring to Steven Shaviro's *Connected, or What It Means to Live in the Network Society* (2003) and Patrick Jagoda's *Network Aesthetics* (2016), though only the latter explicitly attributes the apothegm to Forster. Making Forster's dream, desire, ethical prescription, and aesthetic program the first node in an intellectual history of theorizing networks in turn makes the network a thing of the twentieth century and beyond, of the new medias and technologies that would retroactively reveal the Edwardian novel as a revolutionized and perpetually eclipsed form. "Only connect!" becomes "everything is connected." A command for the future becomes a *fait accompli*. At the same time, Jagoda acknowledges—in a paradigmatically expansive account of the capacities of network thinking—that the accomplishment entailed by the phrase "everything is connected" is much harder to pin down, let alone decipher:

> It simultaneously connotes a felt fact of contemporary life, a metaphysical discovery, and a scientific paradigm; a banal catchphrase of globalization, an ideology of digital media, and a fantasy of social sublimity; a provocation that surges forth from experiences of alienation, a reaction formation developed through encounters with irreducible complexity, and a corollary of a control society; a corporate slogan, a paranoid pronouncement, and a realization of apophenia; an idea that burgeons from deep human bonds, a sense that rises out of ephemeral affinities, and an impossible desire for ambient intimacy; an epistemological foundation, an experience of diaspora, and a utopian impulse; and perhaps still, as in *Howards End*, a spiritual conviction.[1]

The pre-theoretical, affective resonances of connectivity and the ideological sources of networking as an action seem to spread all over the sociopolitical map. Are networks, so often invoked in and referenced by catchphrases, primarily fantasy objects, control mechanisms, utopian horizons, or just basic descriptions of mundane interactions?

Network theorists have offered just about every kind of account and analysis. The concept figures in nearly every scholarly field imaginable, each laying claim to networks in their own terms. These fields include anthropology, biology, computer science, economics, engineering, geography, geology, linguistics, mathematics, neuroscience, political science, sociology, and, of course, every type and subset of media analysis, from prehistoric to broadcast and Internet. Each of these domains appeals to a form of flexible structure abstract enough to flit across disciplinary and practical boundaries but reducible to different, unshared base materials—neurons, people, money, morphemes and phonemes, transmitters and receivers. Before assuming every type of network is analogous to every other, one is thrown back on that notion of *structure*—nodes and links and degrees—one capacious enough to apply all over the place, to reveal something meaningful about so many different systems and scales of human and non-human activity.

There are no holistic, summative accounts of "network theory," no comprehensive field guide to its sub-species out there yet. This is not the book to attempt such a thing. At most, it is a prolegomenon to any future attempt, a modestly equipped (and funded) laboratory for gathering those species around an unusually provocative cinematic text. I will proceed as a specimen collector as much as an organizer or curator. There are more direct quotations in this book than in many introductory volumes to more established schools of theory; it is a necessary price to pay when approaching a still ill-defined group of thinkers and thoughts. The diversity of network theories and phenomena studied makes true but now trivial statements like "everything is connected" apply so liberally and so unquestionably. This book's aim is to draw attention, within network theory as a wide system of interdisciplinary scholarship, to the hubs that specifically center aesthetic concerns, especially cinematic ones.

Those hubs cluster in the late twentieth century and are still growing tentacles today. But the word *network* appeared in the English language at least as far back as the sixteenth century, and its early usage was invariably grounded in materials like textiles or metals. "And thou shalt make it into a grate like networke of brass," reads a passage from Exodus in the 1560 Geneva Bible.[2] Right there, networks are at once made things and the making of those things, reticulated structures fashioned from materials like brass or silk, with strands or threads or wires, interwoven and crisscrossed. Network produces networks. The term would only later be applied to natural formations of similar structure. But because "network" refers to a form and its making, a mode of *work* as well as a *net*-like product, history bears out its conceptual expansiveness. Edmund Spenser refers to a spider web as a network in a 1590 poem. Sir Thomas Browne described the "inward parts of man" as a network in 1658, leading to its widespread application as a term for the structures of animal and plant tissue. In 1839, Connop Thirlwall referred to a set of islands as a network in *A History of Greece*. Then, it was further used as a geological and geographical descriptor of mappable natural formations. 1869 saw the word used for railway systems, but only after Ralph Waldo Emerson used the term more abstractly in his 1858 *English Traits* to articulate the extent of the British social system's "artificial" character: "Their law is a network of fictions." The term was first used in the domain of electrical engineering in 1883, when an entry in a professional journal referenced a "network of conductors." Not until 1914 would it be used in the context of wireless broadcasting, when William Atherton Du Puy, in *Uncle Sam's Modern Miracles*, told of a "great network of stations" across the globe "hurl[ing] forth its messages."

From there, the term undergoes extensive specialization. In twentieth-century chemistry, telecommunications, broadcast media, engineering, computing, industrial economics, management theory, social analysis, and theoretical mathematics, "network" would take a wealth of materials, phenomena, and highly specific human endeavors under its purview. I will draw on some of them in this book, since network theory is nothing if not a plurality of associations. It may be nothing *but* that plurality of associations, loosely joined (but joined indeed!) by the form—the network form— every use of the word posits about its objects and the worlds they occupy. A history of usage is not a history of theory. But networks spread just like the word "network" has. Many network theorists would come to celebrate the sprawling reticulation. Which is not to say the embrace was universal.

"Duh!"

From where we sit now, there may be few things more obvious, less worth announcing, than the notion that "we live in a network society." I am not quoting anyone in particular, but a generalized social voice you may have heard too. That bore at the dinner party. That intro to new media studies textbook. Which does not mean the proposition is false. Or that we know exactly what we mean when we say it, or hear it, or nod along in agreement, or respond with a "duh!" It may not even be interesting, to those who already know the film at least a little bit, to call *Nashville* a "network film." If that category means anything to you, you might already throw it into that basket without looking, alongside other Altman ensemble-cast features, popular twenty-first-century hits like Richard Curtis's *Love Actually* (2003), and objects of film student worship like Quentin Tarantino's *Pulp Fiction* (1994). Cinephiles everywhere have their own favorite examples, made in Hollywood or not, made sometime in the past fifty years or not.

The idea that "we live in a network society" may be trivial because it is all-encompassing. Where to even start with it? *Nashville* is the ultimate subject of this book, but I want to begin with another cinematic example. In the ensemble-cast film *I Heart Huckabees* (dir. David O. Russell, 2004), a detective played by Dustin Hoffman gives his client (played by

Jason Schwartzman) a lesson in pop (and prop) metaphysics with the aid of a white blanket: "Say this blanket represents all the matter and energy in the universe." Each person, object, meta-object, or event in existence is a tiny fold on the surface of the blank sheet. "We think everything is separate, limited, I'm over here, you're over there," he continues, "Which is true. But it's not the whole truth. Because we're all connected." The problem is that the film, which embeds Hoffman's monologue as one small fold in *its* fabric, tries to provide support for this thesis by (duh!) having its several apparently separate characters and storylines converge. If everything is connected, though, why insist on it so explicitly? If heard often enough, it can begin to feel like we say "everything is connected" to convince ourselves of something we truly doubt. If all the investigators' cases in *I Heart Huckabees* did not intertwine, would we be moved to think its story world was really, at bottom, made up of a set of isolated individuals without any connective links between them?

But let us say, for now, that everything is indeed connected—everything, to borrow another film's title, everywhere all at once linked together. How far do such propositions go? And, perhaps more importantly, what's the value of such an assertion? *I Heart Huckabees* seems to posit the "we are all connected" form as a kind of self-help doctrine or internalizable mantra to aid human beings as they try to keep living through a meaningless cosmos. Another well-known (and confusingly Oscar'd) network film, Paul Haggis's *Crash* (2004), uses the "inevitable collision" device—opening with a literal car crash, but shot through with an expanding series of "crashes" between characters—to bolster its vision of a Los Angeles irreparably riven by racism. Some taglines are just perfect for microwave re-warmed melodrama: "Moving at the speed of life, we are bound to collide with each other." Car crashes, yes, but also homicides, robberies, sexual assaults, verbal insults, and heroic about-faces, all happening across one color line or another. When connection, collision, and crash serve moral ends, network films become liturgical parables, just hard to summarize briskly. Hsuan L. Hsu tries by calling its bumper-to-bumper network of interracial impact a clarion call for "raceless aesthetic," ultimately re-hierarchizing its diverse ensemble of characters by the manner in which they are able to assimilate into American society.[3] Do the film's final wide shots, where even the least connected characters can be seen (by us) to brush past each other, engaging in the little collisions that make up the urban, multiracial everyday, thereby peddle the notion that no matter what our cultural or ethnic or gendered background, we are all part of the same universal social fabric? That beneath all our differences, we are all basically the same? Or does the film end by suggesting that *despite* all our links and glancing moments of contact we remain trapped in our microcultures and headspaces, and that it takes a crisis—like the film itself, perhaps, a crisis of artfully banal Hollywood storytelling—to momentarily reveal the truth of the porousness of those inner spaces? Can we even decide either way?

The larger point is that if everything is connected, surely everything has always been connected. This would mean no specific moral or gnomic existential mantra can be the inevitable conclusion to the network tautology. Can a world in which everything is connected become more connected? Or, if we start representing the world as a network, do we thereby reinforce its network qualities? That would be one justification for network theory in addition to network film, the network novel, and the network video game: by recognizing the networks working and mapping their forms and activities in thought, we complete the networks, tying off the final stitch in their fabrics. Even if networks are nothing new, theorizing them may be, relatively speaking. And making networks while knowing that we are making them may be too. And the identification and valuation of networks is what matters. Luc Boltanski and Eve Chiapello call it "a mode of judgment which, taking it for granted that the world is a network (and not, for e.g., a system, a structure, a market, or a community), offers fulcra for appraising and ordering the relative value of beings in such a world."⁴ The appraising, ordering, and valuing do not happen automatically, but by way of the process of thinking and making in network terms, with the network concept.

This book elucidates the value of networking in cinematic form. It does not try to theorize networks as the name and explanation for how everything, or even the most important things—like cultures, societies, and artworks—necessarily *are* at the expense of all other descriptors (like, say, systems or structures). Neither does it try to provide a survey of all uses or abuses of the network concept. But, with Altman's astonishing *Nashville* at the forefront, it does want to understand what networks are good for. Which means being resourceful about how and why network theory—out of a baggy network of adjacent but weakly affiliated theories—eventually came to be nameable as a semi-unified field of thought. It goes without saying that I believe it is a useful designation for how we might think, read, and experience. But I do not take for granted that it is always so. If it is demonstratively successful in the context of cinema studies, the films we watch and study pick up much of the slack, demonstrating as they proceed in time how networks work—as narrative form, as media, as cognitive model.

Or, put another way: if I have picked the right film and have paid close enough attention to it, I will have offered as much as I can in the way of proof about the legitimacy of network form. But in contextualizing and discussing network theory as such, there is no such primary selection, no DVD to insert. The task is to gather network and network-adjacent concepts and put them into orbit, to see how wide or tight their revolutions around the target—"network theory"—must be. There is as much interpretation in the latter activity as in the former. Which is a good thing. At no point in this book will I try to simply apply network theory *in toto* to *Nashville*, as if one holds all the secrets to the other. Students of film and film theory might already feel the fraudulence of that move anyway. You should not need a white blanket to show how everything around that blanket is connected.

The Rise of Network Cinema

Zooming out, we can start by trying to figure out what network theory is, or we can start by trying to figure out what a network film is. This book's first chapter attempts to do both together, before tracing *Nashville*'s network form more closely in its second. David Bordwell, who baptized these sorts of films "network narratives" in the first place—they do have other names, as we will see—provides a working filmography as of 2008, 200 films that generally fit his conception of network form.[5] Perusing the list, even the devoted cineaste will come across unheard-of titles. And the sheer number of categorizable network films, not to mention adjacent media texts like miniseries, network video games, and new media applications, has swollen considerably since Bordwell published his filmography. There is no small canon, though we may argue for our own network film Hall of Fame classes. This is what happens when a form reaches and breaches a certain threshold of quantity—at what point would it have been unworkable to list all the films structured by the single protagonist-hero's quest? Or the couple's journey to happiness ever after (the end of the movie)? Whether it is reasonable or laughably stupid to try to list every token of a particular type is a good initial test for ascertaining the scale of that type's proliferation.

Bordwell claims that network cinema (at least as a matter of statistical significance) does not really take off until the early 1990s, and he dates the "current vogue" for the form to the years 1993 and 1994. That might be right if we focus on the sheer number of network films produced—there was an explosion in the 1990s, no doubt—but the form had been tested on and off for a long time. Ensemble-cast films had a first heyday in the 1960s, as the declining studio system tried to sell star-studded epics to a distracted public. From the heist-gang-outlaw-buddy films of *Ocean's 11* (1960) and *The Magnificent Seven* (1960) to the Cinerama epic *How the West Was Won* (1963), the madcap *It's a Mad Mad Mad Mad World*

(1963), the all-star roster of *The V.I.P.s* (1963), the Katherine Anne Porter adaptation *Ship of Fools* (1965), the Technicolor *Hotel* (1967), the disaster drama *Airport* (1970), and much in between, alternatives to conventional Hollywood protagonist structures gained in mainstream force. New Hollywood auteurs like Altman upped the ante in the 1970s and laid out their hands for more experimentally minded filmmakers to emulate and react against. I have selected *Nashville* as a focus, then, not just because it is an exceptional network film but because it was a node in a broader congealing of network cinema happening in the wake of the studio system's decline. But the indie 1990s made network form feel inevitable for anyone making movies on the industry's cutting edge. Altman's *Short Cuts* (1993), Michael Haneke's *71 Fragments of a Chronology of Chance* (1994), Atom Egoyan's *Exotica* (1994), Wong Kar-wai's *Chungking Express* (1994), and, of course, Quentin Tarantino's *Pulp Fiction* (1994) set the stylistic standards for contemporary network films.

Isolating two years as the seedbed for a sprout burst would seem to suggest some simple historical cause for the vogue. Bordwell, sensibly, does not offer "a single cause," but "point[s] toward certain preconditions," some internal to the film industry, some not.[6] On one hand: new marketing models for American independent film distribution, a market glut that incentivizes standing out through indie quirk, the huge impact of home-video media and its activation of rewind-and-search viewing, friendly cost structures for hiring ensemble casts, incentives for European Union co-productions to cross national borders and integrate multiplicities. On the other hand: networking concepts gaining steam in culture at large, from the dawn of widespread Internet use to network models for disease contact tracing (with Human Immunodeficiency Virus [HIV] outbreaks the glaring historical example). Maybe postmodern pastiche, or just the wide cultural influence among new filmmaking generations of television sitcoms, long-running ensemble dramas, comic book universes, and speculative fiction genres. Jagoda argues that Bordwell focuses too much on inner-Hollywood and media industry causes, underplaying "the importance of the paradigm shift taking place during these years in the areas of complexity and network science, as well as the mass cultural interest in these new scientific fields."[7] Jagoda's historical claim is that three "roughly parallel" twentieth-century developments "took a programmatic form by the 1990s" and generalized the network concept sufficiently well to give it the explanatory reach it enjoys: (1) the mathematical and scientific innovations that grounded network science; (2) the development of the Internet and its "decentralized information architecture"; and (3) neoliberalism and the postindustrial economy.[8] Bordwell does, however, mention other academic network theories that may have played a role by infiltrating popular discourse—I will return to some of these in the following chapter.

And yet there is a difference, as we will see, between the narrative time of theory and the chronological unfolding of the form (in art, in society) that theory cares about. A society-wide interest in networks may feed the ambitious, forward-thinking artists at work; a growing archive of network narratives may help us notice things about life and storytelling that have been there all along, or for a long while. *Nashville* was a product of the New Hollywood 1970s. It produced its own vogue, albeit one centered around the film itself and a sense of Altman's auteurism rather than the network concept as such. The underrated *Honky Tonk Freeway* of 1981 (directed by John Schlesinger) was tellingly promoted as "*Nashville* on wheels." That film begins by cross-cutting between scenes set in a small Florida tourist town and in seemingly unconnected locations across the United States. The latter follow a series of eccentrics making their way to town, all labeled by their distances from Ticlaw, Florida. The root of the plot network is the campaign led by Ticlaw's mayor, for a freeway exit that would put the town on the map, join it to the interstate network, and connect what is currently an isolated, bypassed node north of Miami to the rest of America. We have an asymmetrical narrative system where one task, led by a charismatic community leader, is juxtaposed with a multiplicity of road movie wanderings or micro-threads. Whether Ticlaw will become a new network hub in the story world parallels the question of whether the character ensemble will be able to come together by the end of the film—both targets coincide, and so therefore does the network plot with its meta-plot. *Honky Tonk Freeway* was one of the biggest box office bombs in Hollywood's post-studio era, but it remains a perfect example of a desire for connectivity, stimulated by its social and economic obstacles (which are also obstacles inherent to the network form), that burst into cultural self-consciousness in the wake of Altman's early 1970s critical successes.

But again, none of this is totally new. Way back in pre-Code 1932, Metro-Goldwyn-Mayer(MGM)'s *Grand Hotel* (dir. Edmund Goulding) opened with a montage scene where a whole cast of guests at the eponymous Berlin hotel phone the outside world, emphasizing and prologuing a then-new film form through accent shots of crisscrossed telephone wires connecting characters to unseen, unheard interlocutors. The hotel's lobby gives the network volume, with a 360-degree reception desk formalizing the hub at the center of the film's interwoven character pathways. Abstract telephonic spatiality and the hotel's central commons meet conceptually, even dialectically, in the film's cuts between isolated individuals in their booths, compartments, and rooms (Garbo: "I want to be alone") and small-world crossings out and about in wide space. The opening montage form, increasing in the rapidity with which telephone conversations cut into one another, gives us a discursive awareness the characters may initially lack. Their private interiors bleed out into the very network their one-way communications rely on and that connects each dramatic monologue to the others. Noise permeates the system, and people think and act at cross-purposes, but what begins as a series of characters locked away in their own booths and boxes progressively thaws into a partially visible totality. While theorists often define networks as radically non-hierarchical, network films help us understand how thinking and perceiving networks depend on a particular sort of narrational omniscience.

The hotel is the network's visible infrastructure, though its truest manifestation is in the ambiguous nowhere space of the operators (who do of course labor somewhere, but where the switchboard room exists relative to the lobby and the telephone booths remains spatially unarticulated). On a meta-narrative level, strain emerges between individuals and network, between the too-short, too-scarce amount of screen time allotted each character and the implied wider world (of industry, of war, of law, of the performing arts). Social spectacle, in *Grand Hotel*, conceals but does not replace interiority.[9] It's a dialectic that determines the size of the networked cast through limitation, with immense stars (Garbo, yes, but also two Barrymores and Joan Crawford) checking in for the narrative equivalent of one-night stays. Edgar G. Ulmer's 1945 location network feature *Club Havana* begins with a wry nod to its predecessor's opening, with calls for table reservations coming in constantly behind the din and music of the bustling nightclub—there are only so many characters that can be let in. Network films have introduced and reintroduced themselves periodically over the course of the medium's history, even as its catalog bunches around the turn of the twenty-first century. Altman would nod to the tradition and its evolution by calling *Nashville* his "Grand Motel."[10]

Network Theory and *Nashville*

When thinking about *Nashville*'s importance as a major node in the evolution of network film, it is worth trying to recapture some of the delightful surprise *Nashville* provoked upon its initial release. Far from the origin of network cinema, it does hold a rightful high place in the history of the now-common form. Its meandering, multi-directional, *noisy* narrative structure—or what many saw as non-structure—was equally exhilarating and frustrating to audiences in 1975, even to those already familiar with Altman's *M*A*S*H** (1970), *McCabe & Mrs. Miller* (1971), and *The Long Goodbye* (1973). Unlike many ensemble-cast, multi-protagonist, intertwined storyline films to come, *Nashville* does not immediately reward viewers' desires to resolve all that initially appeared chaotic and random with a satisfying, if sometimes serendipitous, sense of meaningful narrative unity. This is not to say there are no formal unities achieved. Just that some networks are more centrally unified than others, and the same goes for films composed on network principles.

To get from network theory more broadly to network aesthetics, network cinema, and eventually *Nashville* by itself, I will be progressively narrowing the scale of my focus while keeping the general network concept perpetually in view. The first chapter aims to pull something that has yet to be named, network film theory, out of the sprawling, interdisciplinary discourse of network theory. Ultimately, I aim to show how network theory can assist our understanding of how cinematic narratives work. If networks can model social fields and their information flows, and the network film is one expression of social life, then network theory can help us understand the way cinema is uniquely able to map social bodies and forces larger than traditional narrative forms are typically able to cover. We will have new tools to think through Altman's *Nashville*, and any other network film we happen to connect with.

Notes

1 Patrick Jagoda, *Network Aesthetics* (Chicago: University of Chicago Press, 2016), 7–8.
2 *Oxford English Dictionary*, s.v. "network (*n.*), sense 1," April 2023, https://doi.org/10.1093/OED/8164693999.
3 Hsuan L. Hsu, "Racial Privacy, the L.A. Ensemble Film, and Paul Haggis's *Crash*," *Film Criticism* 31.1–2 (Fall/Winter 2006): 149.

4 Luc Boltanski and Eve Chiapello, *The New Spirit of Capitalism* (London: Verso, 2005), 151.
5 See David Bordwell, *Poetics of Cinema* (New York: Routledge, 2008), 245–50.
6 Ibid., 197.
7 Jagoda, 75.
8 Ibid., 10–11.
9 See Mark Goble's reading of the film in *Beautiful Circuits: Modernism and the Mediated Life* (New York: Columbia University Press, 2010), especially p. 118.
10 See Jan Stuart, *The Nashville Chronicles: The Making of Robert Altman's Masterpiece* (New York: Simon & Schuster, 2000), 22.

CHAPTER 1

What Are Networks?

Seven Bridges, Six Degrees

Allow me to take us back in time for a bit. In 1736, Swiss mathematician Leonhard Euler set out to solve a problem known as the Seven Bridges of Königsberg. The Prussian city of Königsberg, built on the Pregel River, included two midstream islands. Seven bridges connected the banks of the city and its islands together. The question is whether there is any single walking path that crosses each of the seven bridges exactly once. Denizens of Königsberg could (and, apparently, did) try to solve the problem by testing every possible path through the city and across its bridges. But Euler proved that there was, in fact, no such path, and he did so via mathematical proof. The proof was a graph, where all but the relevant details of the problem were excluded, leaving only nodes (representing the four land masses divided by water) and links (representing the seven bridges). None of the details one might notice along the way, when walking the city—the streets that traverse each part of the city, for instance, or the direction of the river's flow—figure into the graph, since in this case all that matters is the connectivity between the nodes. If we replaced the land masses with boats and the bridges with wooden planks thrown down between them, the graph would remain the same provided the relations between each did not shift in the process.

The relations between the relevant layout of the city (its land masses and bridges) and Euler's graph is a primary example of the relations between a network's material substrate and its figure. The Seven Bridges of Königsberg, the problem that led Euler to develop (arguably) the first theorem in what came to be known as graph theory—the mathematical language that describes the properties of networks—was an appropriate jumping-off point in intellectual history because the metaphorical transition from world to diagram was relatively smooth and easy. This network's "Eulerian path," which follows each link once and only once, would have been (if it existed, which it did not) an actual path Euler or anyone else could have walked. But the notion of a path through a network, Eulerian or otherwise, was malleable enough to take on forms less literal than a stroll. It could be applied, mathematically, to purely artificial constructs, as well as naturally occurring and manmade networks in the so-called real world.

How about in fiction? Again, let us start with a provocation as simple and elegant as the Seven Bridges. In 1929, Hungarian writer Frigyes Karinthy published a short story, collected in *Everything is Different* (*Ötvenkét vasárnap*), translated into English as "Chains" or "Chain-Links" (*Láncszemek*). It is very brief. It does not contain much in the way of story at all, reading more like a Nietzschean blend of meditation and parable: "Everything returns and renews itself. The difference now is that the *rate* of these returns has increased, in both space and time, in an unheard-of fashion. Now my thoughts can circle the globe in minutes. Entire passages of world history are played out in a couple of years."[1] The unnamed narrator engages in discussion with some unnamed interlocutors "about whether the world is actually evolving, headed in a particular direction, or whether the entire universe is just a returning rhythm's game, a renewal of eternity."[2] Which leads the group to invent a parlor game:

> One of us suggested performing the following experiment to prove that the population of the Earth is closer together

now than they have ever been before. We should select
any person from the 1.5 billion inhabitants of the Earth—
anyone, anywhere at all. He bet us that, using no more than
five individuals, one of whom is a personal acquaintance, he
could contact the selected individual using nothing except
the network of personal acquaintances.[3]

Here we find Six Degrees of Kevin Bacon's trailhead. The
group of immediate acquaintances hypothesizes that after the
turn of the twentieth century "any inhabitant of our Planet"
is reachable in this way, from the winner of the Nobel Prize
for Literature to "an anonymous riveter at the Ford Motor
Company."[4] It has become easier to be sure of the success of
connecting oneself to a distant other in five links or fewer today;
tracing mutual friends on social media is the simplest method.
But even in 1929, Karinthy's narrator positions himself and
the rest of his species on the former side of a great divide,
between a connected global village and an unconnected one:

Julius Caesar, for instance, was a popular man, but if he
had got it into his head to try and contact a priest from one
of the Mayan or Aztec tribes that lived in the Americas at that
time, he could not have succeeded—not in five steps, not even
in three hundred. Europeans in those days knew less about
America and its inhabitants than we now know about Mars
and its inhabitants.[5]

Mars (and its inhabitants) is neither a random nor a
melodramatic example—eventually humanity will reach
other planets, settle down on them, establish communications
technologies linking them to those still on Earth and maybe
even species beyond our current purview. The world keeps
shrinking, which is the same thing as saying, in current
parlance, that society keeps on networking.

Karinthy's story does not necessarily come down on the side
of network society, does not explicitly celebrate it or view it as
a promising end of history, nor does it obviously rail against it.
But, and this is the story behind the minimal story, its narrator
cannot stop playing the game:

> I am embarrassed to admit—since it would look foolish—that I often catch myself playing our well-connected game not only with human beings, but with objects as well. I have become very good at it. It's a useless game, of course, but I think I'm addicted to it, like a gambler who, having lost all of his money, plays for dried beans without any hope of real gain—just to see the four colors of the cards. The strange mind-game that clatters in me all the time goes like this: how can I link, with three, four, or at most five links of the chain, trivial, everyday things of life? How can I link one phenomenon to another? How can I join the relative and the ephemeral with steady, permanent things—how can I tie up the part with the whole?[6]

Karinthy's narrator sounds a bit like "Actor-Network" theorist Bruno Latour here, incorporating objects animate and inanimate into his picture of a hyper-connected society. But we will come back to Latour. Note, for now, the desire to see through people, objects, things, and everyday phenomena to "the whole," to see through the "relative and the ephemeral" to the "steady" and "permanent." This is a Platonic need, an intuition that seeing connection and tracing relation between elements of mortal life's flux leads the mind to eternal and unchanging realms, the true Being that is the All, the whole. No longer armchair sociology, this is Monday morning metaphysics.

"A Meets B, Then C . . ."

If network thinking easily slides into metaphysics, or generates feelings of a sacred connectedness of everything, nothing prevents us from returning to the basics. When we consider narratives as networks, we usually assume its nodes are its characters. The chain links that connect a narrated story together are primarily people (though as we will see, not *only* people). David Bordwell breaks down the plot structure of

Lotte Svendsen's 2004 film *What's Wrong With This Picture?* (*Tid til Forandring*) with an algebraic schema:

> So A meets B, then C, then D. B and C already know each other. Through C we get to meet E, and through D we get to meet F—even though A doesn't know them. The film opens up a social structure of acquaintance, kinship, and friendship beyond any one character's ken. The narration gradually reveals the array to us, attaching us to one character, then another. And the actions springing from this social structure aren't based on tight causality. The characters, however they're knit together, have diverging purposes and projects, and these intersect only occasionally—often accidentally.[7]

Bordwell's ABC's suggest interchangeability, even if that is not quite his intention. But to some degree, the characters in a network film are interchangeable—not as individual people in the story world, to be sure, but as bearers of dramatic importance. As narrative agents, their coexistence flattens the hero-sidekick, major-minor, lead-support topology into a democracy of the middle. The lead ensemble of a network film leads *as* an ensemble. The film's "social structure" does not privilege the causal agency of a single protagonist or antagonist, and A, B, C, or Z can take on different narratological roles across story threads—central to one arc of action, secondary to another, and completely irrelevant to yet another.

Evan Smith calls network form in film "thread structure." "Each thread is a separate main story and all threads have roughly the same dramatic weight."[8] But even as each thread retains dramatic importance, it is as a member of a textual democracy, casting no more than one vote for preeminence. Due to the conventional limitations of the feature film's runtime, each story thread is more abbreviated than a standard linear plot throughline. Filmmakers must decide whether to elide plot points or dramatic acts in a character's story thread—having events take place off-screen, behind the spectators' backs—or shorten the story's path significantly. Sometimes plot resolution is withheld altogether. It is the difference between "Send your hero up a tree, throw rocks at him, get him down from the tree" and "Send several characters up short trees, maybe bushes; Throw rocks at each, or maybe just look at the rocks, or just wave threateningly; Get some of the characters down, leave some up, and the others...they just disappear."[9] One of Smith's examples is Mia Wallace (Uma Thurman) in Quentin Tarantino's *Pulp Fiction*. Her romantic storyline with Vincent Vega (John Travolta) begins *in utero*, titillates, rushes headlong into overdose crisis, and is unceremoniously severed with an agreement between Mia and Vincent to stop seeing each other and never mention any of it ever again. The story does not end; it merely stops.

But how relative are distinctions like ending versus stopping, long versus short, standard plotline versus thread? Most complex narratives have a plenitude of characters, locations, and dramatic objectives. How many novels or feature films (not to mention modern musicals) really reduce to Aristotelian unities, to a hero's or heroine's single-minded adventure? Are there any network-less narratives? Defining narrative forms on spectrums, though, does not inherently call the basic existence of the forms into question. We can helpfully define network narratives in general and network films in particular as texts that produce their own theory of networks, by making the node-link structure that always already inheres in narrative, as its oft-unspoken basis, more obvious, more visible, more perspicuous.

Kristin Thompson's narratology of classical Hollywood cinema can serve as the baseline from which network narratives tend to depart. The most common narrative structure in Hollywood film, Thompson claims, consists of four acts of similar length: the setup, complicating action, development, and climax. In most cases, these acts make up a "unified narrative," wherein "a cause should lead to an effect and that effect in turn should become a cause for another effect, in an unbroken chain across the film."[10] Each section's plot consistency is oriented around the protagonist's desire, which provides the narrative's "forward impetus." The Hollywood protagonist is "goal oriented," desiring someone or something, and those goals center the "main lines of action."[11] The main character's pursuit(s) give each act its narrative identity, in other words, with the main storyline shifting as their aims or tactics shift. The turns in the action that join each act, connecting while separating them like a threshold between expansive rooms, are formal correlates for the unfolding of the protagonist's pursuit as it meets the diegetic world set up by the film, a world grounded by linear causality. Complicating this narratological picture somewhat is Thompson's insistence that classical Hollywood cinema tends to have two main lines of action, one almost always romantic, but both lines parallel each other and follow the four-act course together in time. The two main lines are "bound up together," though the "means for resolving each" may be different, as in professional and private storylines which may ultimately intersect (the serendipitous moment) or require separate resolution-events in the film's climactic section.[12]

Network narratives may dispense with goal-oriented action, but they also might not. Narratives with clear protagonists or central pairs magnetize its discourse and its presented plot around the goals of a single person, or a very small group of people close to a person who quickly emerges as the focal point of our attention. The network narrative's *sine qua non* is that the protagonist structure is dispersed among several personae, leveling the distinction between major and minor characters. María del Mar Azcona considers network films, or what she also calls mosaic films, a variant of the "multi-protagonist film" (which she takes to be not just a form but a genre). She lists seven narrative and thematic "multi-protagonist" conventions or ranges of conventions, all of which we can generally associate with network narratives (and which I will abbreviate). Multi-protagonist films:

1. feature a broad spectrum of characters involved in different storylines;
2. may be independent of one another, can crisscross regularly, or be framed by each other;

3. may be narrated in tandem or sequentially, sometimes (but not always) structured around a common space or location;
4. tend to concentrate on characters at the expense of tight lines of action, substituting coincidence, chance, and group dynamics for straightforward causality;
5. establish unlikely connections between characters in ostensibly different storylines through synchronic narrative structures, often linked thematically to some commentary on human interconnection;
6. may give the impression, given the emphasis on chance and coincidence, that less is happening to the characters than we might otherwise expect;
7. by presenting a plurality of differing, even contradictory points of view, suggest the complexity and multidimensionality of the primary thematic concerns, substituting open, circular, or multiple endings for traditional moral resolutions and plot closures.[13]

A helpful list. But as we see, eliminating centrality and spreading narrational focus among a group does not necessarily entail a specific value organizing how the story threads must be structured in time, or whether the plurality need cohere in the modes or manners of their telling. That is a matter of investigation on another level of the narrative discourse: the thematic or stylistic coherence or lack thereof might communicate something about what the network form is *for* in any one case. How much is the network structure a means for control or for chance? There is no answer that can suffice ahead of time, for the whole category.

Network Sociology

Let us imagine network narratives as applied sociology. If early modern thinkers like Euler theorized rudimentary networks as mathematical thought experiments, in between those initial provocations and twentieth-century graph theory came the rise of academic analysis of the structure of human cultures and societies. The ostensible messiness, contingency, and formlessness of social interactions presented a challenge to be overcome by sharper methodological tools. Émile Durkheim, for instance, a fountainhead of the twentieth-century discipline of sociology, aimed to establish a professional theoretical edifice and set of methods proper to an autonomous science. In *The Rules of the Sociological Method* (1895), Durkheim defines and studies "social facts," a set of phenomena that had been grouped to that point "without much precision."[14] The "exact field of sociology" according to Durkheim "embraces one single, well defined group of phenomena. A social fact is identifiable through the power of external coercion which it exerts or is capable of exerting upon individuals."[15] Social facts are "every way of acting, whether fixed or not, capable of exerting over the individual an external constraint; or: which is general over the whole of a given society whilst having an existence of its own, independent of its individual manifestations."[16] Social facts do not reduce to the actions of any individual member of society—they exist on their own, apart from any individual—and yet "exert" constraints on individual actions.

Durkheim's "social fact" was a legitimate if tentative conceptual move toward social network theory, not in name or in its finest details but in those broad strokes that often characterize intellectual history's paradigm shifts. It was posited in the wake of nineteenth-century utilitarian and liberal social theories, in which society was thought to be largely the byproduct of individual decisions and actions. Curiously, Durkheimian sociology was—again, broad genealogical strokes—a return to pre-eighteenth-century notions of selves as nexuses of social positions rather than free, self-constructed individuals. Indeed, liberal social theory passed down from Adam Smith and his contemporaries was grounded in the first place by a theory of individual subjectivity, affect, and conscious awareness. Smith's sense of the social was entirely pre-network thinking in at least one important way. While he famously depicts human feelings like sympathy as levers that "carry us beyond our own person," into an understanding of the inextricable links between people that make up a social world, he argues that our senses "never did, and never can, carry us beyond our own person, and it is by the imagination only that we can form any conception of what are [another person's, a suffering brother's] sensations."[17] The imagination is what carries us beyond our selves, and while this is nothing new in the theory of sympathy, Smith tries to establish that imagination is self-centered, self-motivated, and so sympathy is a reflection not of the power of links between people but of their weakness. "As we have no immediate experience of what other men feel, we can form no idea of the manner in which they are affected, but by conceiving what we ourselves would feel in the like situation." We are always thinking of ourselves, stuck in our own consciousness and responsive to its experiential history. When I feel your pain, I really feel my own. Our sympathetic bonds with other people are powerful self-projections.

Imagine the entire fabric of society was built out of these sorts of attempts at sympathetic projection. It would mean that while people are aware of other people around them, and can relate to them (and to a lesser extent, could relate to people who are part of cultures less scrutable to their own sense of how life is lived and felt, and to an even lesser extent could relate to animals living among and around them), society is really a just large set of atomistic projections confined to individuals' inner-conscious minds. Durkheim was hardly the first major thinker to challenge such notions (see: Marx, for one).[18] The sociology of networks arose with a negative claim that grounds its positive hypotheses: society should not be thought of as a byproduct of collisions between atomistic individual consciousnesses. For Durkheim, sociology must be sharply distinguished from psychology:

> Social facts differ not only in quality from psychical facts; *they have a different substratum,* they do not

evolve in the same environment or depend on the same conditions. This does not mean that they are not in some sense psychical, since they all consist in ways of thinking and acting. But the states of the collective consciousness are of a different nature from the states of the individual consciousness; they are representations of another kind. The mentality of groups is not that of individuals; it has its own laws.[19]

It is telling that Durkheim illustrates the type difference between individual and collective consciousness through a chemical analogy. In chemistry we tend to accept as uncontroversial things that appear to go against common sense when applied to social life. "Whenever elements of any kind combine, by virtue of this combination they give rise to new phenomena. One is therefore forced to conceive of these phenomena as residing, not in the elements, but in the entity formed by the union of these elements."[20] There is a brute point, at both chemical and social scales, where "life cannot be split up," where the phenomenon in question—biological life in the cell, social life between individual people—cannot be located in any one variable of the equation of interaction. And yet it emerges nonetheless.

Durkheim's *Suicide* (1897) examines one social fact in detail. And suicide is the perfect illustration of Durkheim's attempt at a Copernican revolution in social thought because it appears to be the ultimate existential choice, a radically private one—to be or not to be (?), Hamlet asks, and can answer only by wandering the labyrinth of his own consciousness. If Durkheim can show that suicide is a social fact with social causes, he will justify sociological thinking at a very basic level.[21] He sets about alienating Smithian social analysis from itself by flooding its motivating, intentional engine with external causes. Durkheim's four types of suicide—egoistic, altruistic, anomic, and fatalistic—refer to individual states and feelings, but are ultimately formed *as types* by hydraulic relationships between social groups' levels of integration (their structures of bondedness) and senses of moral regulation (normative prescriptions on behavior). Ultimately, he provides statistical and corresponding intuitionistic accounts of suicide rates broken down along several social-group axes: by gender, sexual and conjugal relationships, family structure, religious affiliation, occupation, and more.

The importance of statistics to Durkheim's analysis of social facts can hardly be overstated. Not only did it justify sociological claims as an empirical science with repeatable methodologies, it also provided a means for distributing law-like regularities collectively, unbinding descriptions from the atomistic individual, allowing for the conceptualization of society as an unfolding set of probable phenomena. If one can begin to think of social laws, which generate social facts, as operating probabilistically—that is, not as an ironclad, deterministic guarantee for a state of mind, pattern of behavior, or act, but as a matter of relative frequency or expectation—one sees a way toward thinking of the social world as a network, as a web of relationships grouped into clusters of family resemblances and linked across differences rather than isolated from the different. Link structures in the social network can then be conceived as a matter of form, as in the distinction between what Durkheim calls mechanical and organic solidarity. Mechanical solidarity describes a society where integration arises from the homogeneity of its members, where collective consciousness dominates the individual, and where the division of labor among members is minimal. Organic solidarity, associated with modern social forms, is networked in a more composite fashion, with the social fabric stitched together through a complex division of labor, with a heterogeneous mix of groups and spheres of activity, and with less determination (or domination) of individual consciousness by the collective.

Durkheim's categories, like incomplete sketches, suggest key distinctions proper to network analysis while retaining the homeliness of now-classical sociological theory. He does not typically figure into the story contemporary network theorists tell about their subject matter. Sociological rivals like Gabriel Tarde get the plaudits of the then-ignored but now-celebrated subversive. Durkheim's work is often confined to a stray footnote, giving off the odor of stale mildew from the back of a vintage armoire. What marks the transition into a mode of thinking that registers as, more precisely, network theory, especially when, as Alexander R. Galloway and Eugene Thacker put it, "the idea of connectivity is so highly privileged today that it is becoming more and more difficult to locate places or objects that don't, in some way, fit into a networking rubric"?[22] And how does a budding network theory of society—not to mention of biological organisms or communicational media systems—inform our attunement toward aesthetics and artworks that develop or adapt network form as a narrative strategy or experiment?

Network Formalism

Caroline Levine's analysis of network form begins with a problem, that the use of networks in cultural studies generally relies on an opposed yet omnipresent concept: "it is the relation of networks and wholes that allow us to grasp culture as an object of study."[23] One the one hand, "it is the wholeness of culture that allows its network of crisscrossing connections to become perceptible in the first place." From this perspective, which Levine attributes to certain anthropologists and New Historicists, only bounded forms can contain networks. On the other hand, many theorists emphasizing processes of globalization hold that "networks are the forms that rupture or defy enclosed totalities and allow us to understand border-crossing circulations and transmissions." Levine asks, like many network theorists before her, whether networks are bounded or unbounded, contained or uncontainable. A formalist approach to networks answers this question best because it focuses our attention on threshold encounters between bounded wholes and branching reticulations.

Network formalism, then, keeps one eye on the capacity for expansiveness networks afford by definition and in theory and another on the imposed rules or infrastructural limitations that bind expansion in practice. A Local Area Network (LAN) establishes a mesh between a finite number of computers that occupy a limited spatial region, like an office building or a school. Levine also mentions kinship networks, tree topologies expansive in principle by way of marriage, reproduction, adoption, and less-traditional groupings and sub-topologies (for instance, queer kinship topologies that might differ diagrammatically from the familial norm) but also regulated by wider social institutions and conventions, like the state which issues marriage licenses or incentivizes/disincentivizes adoption or reproduction, churches or religious bodies that pronounce edicts on allowable practices, and more implicit social norms and prohibitions that prune kinship networks into topiary shapes the neighborhood association approves of. There are also physical or cartographical frontiers certain networks are hard pressed to cross. Levine refers to transportation networks that require infrastructure funding to realize its expansion, or diplomatic finagling to extend across national borders, or an entirely different geographical or geological landscape than whatever is currently available.[24]

Networks are imbricated meshes rather than simple, bounded, and consistent wholes. Think something out of a Calvinoesque fantasy—multiple cities overlapping each other so that they share the same geographical space, a vertiginous alternative to the fortified burg. Or just imagine Charles Dickens's London. We might know the modern city to be a network of networks, but the realist novel can formalize that fact and present it. Law offices, chancery, financial corporations, train stations, curiosity shops, debtors' prisons, factories, street encampments, estates, and townhouses—all conceived as diegetic nodes connecting multiple plots, simultaneous events, character groups. Dickens, from *The Pickwick Papers* to *Bleak House*, *Little Dorrit*, and *Our Mutual Friend*, multiplies the novelist's cast, its familial hubs, its scenic locations, its object circulations, and the sheer number of possibly relevant causes for narrative incidents. Sprawl in the world demands sprawl in novelistic form, and nineteenth-century realism—from Dickens to Eliot, Balzac to Zola, Flaubert to Tolstoy—maps totalities by networking its story world. Focalization on the life paths of single or small groups of characters forms the main spine of novelistic history, but the rise of larger network novels in the mid-nineteenth century furthered the distribution of action beyond dramatic unities which characterized the rise of the novel out of novellas. Tolstoy's *War and Peace* might be the apex of this developmental counter-logic, with its enormous range of well-defined social worlds in addition to its impressive (or impressively confusing) character list.

What happens when you map cities as they appear in novels, or across a series of fictions? Franco Moretti's *Atlas of the European Novel* does just that with Balzac's Paris of the *Comédie Humaine* and Dickens's London of *Our Mutual Friend*, placing characters in specific locations, seeing how they cluster on the map and form social groups, where they go, the degree to which they move or stay in place, whether and how individuals and their social groups interact, where they meet. "Every meeting place, in Balzac, is also a space of exclusion: open to some, and closed to others."[25] Perhaps it is only through cartography of this sort that one can see where "invisible class lines," articulated in fictions by the sorting of a character system, truly fall, how they are marked in the fiction's fabula.[26] Novelistic network maps like Moretti's skim data from the temporal stream of a narrative and represent it spatially, synchronically, as a virtual plan invisible from inside the unfolding narrative. But as a series, literary maps can articulate the processual unfolding of a fictional network, the "rhythm of [its] narrative pattern," tracking the storyworld expansion of a serialized novel like *Our Mutual Friend*, adding a space or two with every installment, and jumping around the city from scene to scene, "from the Thames to the West End, to Limehouse, to Holloway, to Wegg's lonely street corner . . . a 'mosaic or worlds,' yes, but whose tiles have been randomly scattered."²⁷ A series of urban sub-systems that might just, if you're patient enough to build the map out, form a larger system: for Dickens, as in many of his huge novels, scattered families ultimately reconstituted, distributed modern life reclaimed and redeemed by the counter-logic of the family romance.²⁸

The pressure of expansion in the Dickensian network novel never goes away, and his great big works pose questions to the future of the form and its politics, like in *Bleak House*:

> What connexion can there be, between the place in Lincolnshire, the house in town, the Mercury in powder, and the whereabout of Jo the outlaw with the broom. . . . What connexion can there have been between many people in the innumerable histories of the world, who, from opposite sides of great gulfs, have, nevertheless, been very curiously brought together!²⁹

Of course Jo, the impoverished, illiterate urchin with the broom, "sweeps his crossing all day long, unconscious of the link, if any link there be." But we are not Jo; we can read. If anything, reading Dickens we are more like his aptly-named circulating messenger Lorry, from *A Tale of Two Cities*—imaginatively, sympathetically mobile, shuffling to and fro and clinching connections across distances. And as much as we might identify with a character in a film or text—or be pressured to, even uncomfortably, like with Scottie Ferguson in Alfred Hitchcock's *Vertigo*—we are not them. We know more; we connect more freely. That's fiction.

From the apex of nineteenth-century realism to the modernist and postmodernist twentieth century, network forms change but hardly disappear. If anything, they just become more self-conscious over time. Intersecting lives are treated less as a novelistic requirement and more like one possible theme to foreground and explore. One would expect as much in the century of globalized capital, world wars, anti-colonial struggle, and international mass media and communications. The network form in literature truly becomes global, most obviously in the short story cycle—Joyce's *Dubliners* (1914) and Anderson's *Winesburg, Ohio* (1919) are merely two influential starting points—but also exemplified by novels like Thomas Mann's *Buddenbrooks* (1901), Li Baojia's *Officialdom Unmasked* (1903), John Dos Passos's *Manhattan Transfer* (1925), William Faulkner's *As I Lay Dying* (1930), Virginia Woolf's *The Waves* (1931), Camilo José Cela's *The Hive* (1950), Patrick White's *Riders in the Chariot* (1961), Naguib Mahfouz's *Miramar* (1967), Gabriel García Márquez's *One Hundred Years of Solitude (*1967), Thomas Pynchon's *Gravity's Rainbow* (1973), E. L. Doctorow's *Ragtime* (1975), Salman Rushdie's *Midnight's Children* (1981), Toni Morrison's *Jazz* (1992), Don DeLillo's *Underworld* (1997), Jennifer Egan's *A Visit from the Goon Squad* (2011), Imran Coovadia's *Tales of the Metric System* (2014), and Min Jin Lee's *Pachinko* (2017). Just like network films after 1990, it is hard to pick a large handful of texts and present them as a single cluster of representative examples.

Levine's primary text is the critically lauded and recognizably Dickensian HBO series *The Wire* (2002–8). TV, or whatever counts as television today, still leads the way in probing the capacities of network narration. There are easier examples at hand. During the 1990s indie network film explosion, *The Simpsons* (1989–forever) served as cultural weathervane with its celebrated "22 Short Films About Springfield" (1996). That's one storyline per minute, though there are in fact only twenty-one vignettes, which range in length from about :30 to 2:30. Staff writers put their favorite characters into a hat and drew assignments, replicating the narrative chanciness they aimed to produce. Numerous *Pulp Fiction* allusions ground the episode's network form in historical time (the Royale with Cheese, the Gold Watch storyline). The frame narrative involves Bart and Milhouse wondering whether interesting things ever happen in Springfield. The simple lesson learned, of course, is that they do. Another essential 1990s sitcom, *Seinfeld* (1989–98), uses bottle episodes with smaller-world network structures to suggest something like the opposite. Famously described as a "show about nothing," *Seinfeld*'s New York network episodes explore the all-too-typical travails of late twentieth-century first-world life, with a stand-up comedian's neurotic disposition toward the obsessive or absurd. Jerry, George, Elaine, and Kramer are childish adult buddies in that 1990s sitcom fashion—a loosely chosen friend-family, they are an in-group whose weaker social ties to the society that judges them harshly form the structural comedy of the show's episodic plots. Several famous bottle episodes heighten the level of self-reflection toward the group's entwinement with New York social life. They lose each other searching for their car in a mall parking garage; each transfer onto different subway lines and play out the rest of their days based on the people they run into; they struggle to meet up and sit together at the same midtown movie showing. None of these plots would work to such clockwork perfection if they were set just a decade later, when the characters would all have cell phones (maybe the hipster doofus Kramer would live without one on principle, and they would all lose reception in the subway episode, but still). *Seinfeld* lives in the sweet spot where small social networks clash against the pressures of late capitalist frivolity and ennui, but are not yet completely dissolved into the trackable, data-driven networks of social media or mobile telecommunications.

Network Imaginaries

In *Network Aesthetics,* Patrick Jagoda argues that "the problem of global connectedness cannot be understood, in our historical present, independently of the formal features of a network imaginary," which he defines as "the complex of material infrastructures and metaphorical figures that inform our experience with and our thinking about the contemporary social world."[30] Networks are both material and imaginary, infrastructural and figural, literal and metaphorical. Departing from, among other terminals, Fredric Jameson's theory of cognitive mapping, of the subject's mental schema of social and global totalities, Jagoda approaches network form though an aesthetic of contemporary life—of (post-)postmodernism, late capitalism, globalization, digital connectivity. His account begins and ends with gaming, emphasizing the participatory aspect of networks.

One challenge of network thinking (or thinking networks) is getting their material and metaphorical aspects straight. Looking again at the network etymology glossed in this book's introduction, one sees an oscillation between literal, figurative, and newly literal uses of the term. The figure becomes literal or infrastructural over time, incorporating new net-like substrates (made of animal tissue, railroad tracks, laws, messages) into its growing definition. When we imagine networks by abstracting material substrates into diagrams or luminous web-like images with shining nodes, we move in the direction of figure. In grasping the visual form as a figure for understanding a complex network, even if obsolete beyond an infinitesimal slice of time, we participate in the expansion of the network imaginary, furthering the explanatory value of the concept. Expanding the network concept as a matter of figure or form generates a network aesthetic, a way of seeing, drawing, and thinking, that can be deployed in and beyond traditional artforms.

But as a matter of socioeconomic history, the exploding flexibility and circulation of the network concept as such, Jagoda argues, "is connected closely to the expansion of US neoliberalism and finance capitalism, as well as resistances to it."[31] Many network theorists essentially agree. To turn the screw further, the (neoliberal) network imaginary contributes to the expansion of finance capitalism, "connected" to it in the sense of reproducing many of its ideological commitments and self-images. Decentralization, distribution, flexibility, flow, nonlinearity, bottom-up processes, rhizomatic deterritorialization—all name elements of neoliberalism's unfolding process of global liberation, its anti-authoritarianism, its contribution to a cultural pluralism unleashed by deregulation. Manuel Castells describes a "new economy," a new network economy, which "emerged in the last quarter of the twentieth century on a worldwide scale," one which is "informational, global, and networked":

> It is *informational* because the productivity and competitiveness of units or agents in this economy (be it firms, regions, or nations) fundamentally depend upon their capacity to generate, process, and apply efficiently knowledge-based information. It is *global* because the core activities of production, consumption, and circulation, as well as their components (capital, labor, raw materials, management, information, technology, markets) are organized on a global scale, either directly or through a network of linkages between economic agents. It is *networked* because, under the new historical conditions, productivity is generated through and competition is played out in a global network of interaction between business networks (emphasis is in original).[32]

A global network of networks, in other words, emerging as an effect of "the information technology revolution" of the twentieth century. Starr Roxanne Hiltz and Murray Turoff's 1978 *Network Nation* was its late capitalist, pre-Internet prophecy, a guide to and policy analysis for the inevitable future of human communication via computer conferencing, which affords (if we do not regulate it out of existence, they worry) the possibility of a Habermasian utopia where the cost of information approaches zero, where the democratic exchange of ideas occurs angelically and without discriminatory barriers controlling the conversations, where bodies cease to hold us back. Hiltz and Turoff were IT gnostics, ahead of their time and less mystical than they may have initially appeared, predicting the end of hard materiality in communication, the clunky apparatuses of corded telephones and paper mailers. Castells elsewhere describes the network economy's flowing flipside, its powerfully virtual financial markets, as "outside anyone's control... become a sort of automaton, with sudden movements that do not follow a strict economic logic, but a logic of chaotic complexity."[33] How does such uncontrolled and uncontrollable financial flow, such sublime automated chaos, become an exciting prospect, rather than a horrifying, monstrous one?

Galloway's answer is that decentralized network society is *not* a society that has evacuated control (as we might gather simply by noting that Paul Baran was discovering the security benefits of mesh-like distribution while on the RAND Corporation's payroll during the Cold War, serving a military-industrial function like many mid-century network researchers did). Quite the opposite, in fact. One might speculate that it is because control still exists in and through network form that "chaotic complexity" can be imagined as a source or symptom of liberation. "Protocol," Galloway's keyword, is a management style or "principle of organization native to computers in distributed networks."[34] He embarks from Gilles Deleuze's essay "Postscript on Control Societies" (1990), which defined the titular societies as succeeding disciplinary societies, where individuals "are always going from one closed site to another, each with its own laws."[35] First the family, then the school, the barracks, the factory, the hospital, and even the prison. Discipline means enclosure, confinement, institutionalization, lockdown, rigid schedules, hard borders. Michel Foucault's *Discipline and Punish* provides a guide to its panoptic apparatuses, which make individuals and wield power over them by isolating, fixing, and examining their bodies. Observation and command in disciplinary societies establish central norms one can voluntarily conform to or attempt to transgress; the result are regimes of normality and abnormality. Control is more fluid, where our movements and activities are not so much physically bounded as they are channeled, grooved, guided, tracked, or mapped. Control societies take fewer prisoners (at least in principle) but gather more information. If enclosures are social "molds," controls are what Deleuze calls "modulation," distributed further over time and space and harder to experience or even notice on the part of the controlled party. The molds do not just shake and shimmy like Jell-O but ooze and transform, "continually changing from one moment to the next, or like a sieve whose mesh varies from one point to another."[36] Power is no longer exercised primarily on "individuals" or their position in a "mass" but on "dividuals" who are members of "samples, data, markets, or '*banks*,'" each of which are managed by codes regulating levels of access to information.[37] The social units in question are networked phenomena Deleuze and Félix Guattari call assemblages, collections of heterogeneous but articulated phenomena—bodies, rhythms, actions, passions, signs. Not "me" as a simple bounded body with a stable identity that can be molded directly or categorized as an abnormal type, in other words, but a roving data nexus, "me—my bank accounts—my consumption habits—my medical history—my voting patterns—my Instagram follows."

Disciplinary societies, then, produce mass individuation, modeled on the subjectivity of confined interiority. Control societies code everything, allowing subjects to break their molds without exiting the reach of programmatic assessment and tracking. Information flows. As Wendy Hui Kyong Chun puts it, "Digital language makes control systems invisible: we no longer experience the visible yet unverifiable gaze but a network of nonvisualizable digital control."[38] Control is a constant obsession of contemporary network theorists because of its invisibility, the way it creeps into digital networks that ostensibly work to open the freedom of information and access to a global(ized) village. Control is network theory's ambivalent inheritance from the domain of cybernetics, the massively influential twentieth-century field—for theory, industry, marketing, the military, and the artworld each—for studying the non-linear control systems inherent to both automated machines and living organisms. Norbert Wiener defined cybernetics, in the title of his field-defining book, as the scientific study of "control and communication in the animal and machine."[39] An outgrowth of a broader cultural interest in information flow, from Claude Shannon's influential work in telecommunications and wartime cryptanalysis forward, cybernetics models the recursive feedback mechanisms of information within natural and mechanical systems, the way relations between informational input and output create self-governing pathways rather than sheer noisy chaos (and, in information theory more broadly, the ratio between signal and noise, or meaningful information and random variation, becomes the foundational relation upon which all other epistemic conditions are built). In the wake of cybernetics, theorizing networks, or non-linear systems in which a change to any node cascades into changes across the larger fabric, becomes at least partly a matter of considering how feedback controls the shifts in different network forms. And without ever positing a central intelligence or subject guiding every interaction, signal, or response across the network ahead of time.

Chun mines the tension between freedom and control (or, stylized, "control-freedom") in the Internet age, a relation she claims is non-oppositional. On the one hand, the Internet establishes what Tiziana Terranova calls an "open architecture," an informational topology "that tends towards the production of a smooth, open and unbounded space."[40] There is no limit, in principle, to the number of subnetworks an open architecture can accommodate, and the distribution of agency it allows (by easing reliance on centralized command nodes) leads to a "continuous expansion and modification" of the unbounded network that parallels the newfound autonomy of users' navigational pathways through it.[41] But the agency offered to individuals by the Internet is grounded by implicit submission to a wide range of controls operating behind the network's visible screen. The freedom to travel through fiber optic space depends on a prior yielding of control: the free act of browsing a webpage depends on information submission, like your Internet Protocol (IP) address, browser preferences, and userdomain, usually giving your physical location away. You are logged in to a network of other users, participating in an exchange of information whether you know it or not. The Internet solicits uncanny Faustian bargains, asking us to give up agency here for informational gains there.

If Chun's control-freedom dialectic sounds like an intricate science fiction, maybe it is, in a sense. Steven Shaviro's vision of our networked society is a tenuous series of speculative descriptions of a world that "seems on the verge of being absorbed into the play of science fiction novels and films."[42] His theory of (cyber-)network society *is* science fiction, emerging through a series of Adornian aphorisms that landscape twenty-first-century life as one big, connected, thoroughly commercialized theme park existing outside history, in an eternal present of half-satisfied desire. Shaviro's model for the network society is depicted in K. W. Jeter's *Noir,* in a virtual nocturnal zone called the Wedge, which sometimes "seems to overlay the real world, a spectral double of its streets and buildings and private spaces," and sometimes "seems to lie in an actual spatial location, like the red-light district of an older city."[43] The Wedge is a zone of transgression and disavowed pleasure, into which human beings send their avatars, humanoid androids called prowlers, who experience those pleasures and transmit them back to their owners. In the gap between the proxy experience and the transmitted memory that feels now like it was always mine lies the supplemental link between the actual and the virtual. For Shaviro, what it means to live in the network society is to rely on the background humming of virtual worlds for any coherent sense of the actual. Chun would likely agree: the networks we use also use us; we depend on our digital prowlers as much as they depend on us for their existence.

Are we approaching techno-utopia or techno-horror? Tech futurists get giddy at the specter of what Adam Greenfield calls "ubiquitous computing," where "processing power" becomes "distributed throughout the environment" through a "diverse ecology of devices and platforms," and "power and meaning" becomes "more a property of the network than of any single node, and that network is effectively invisible."[44] But the ubiquity Greenfield predicts suggests something so ordinary and un-sci-fi about network control. About the progressive banality of information technology and the culture of flexible labor conditions under what we might call post-industrialism, neoliberalism, or postmodernity as a cultural designation for late capitalism. David Harvey is one of the go-to theorists for this dimension, namely the labor conditions inherent to "the crisis of Fordism" and the financialization process inherent to the late twentieth century's long economic downturn.[45] Decentralized production, networks of sub-contractors and casual labor markets, hyper-lean supply systems, hyper-quick turnovers and reprogrammings, digitalized and affect-driven services, gigs instead of stable jobs. Is network flexibility a source of liberation or the guarantor of new cultures of exploitation?

Framing Sprawl

Networks stretch and spread; it's just what they do, by force of habit if not will. But there are many ways of "forming" networks, of making them *appear* within limits, cinematically or otherwise. As Henry James put it in his preface to the New York Edition of *Roderick Hudson*, "Really, universally, relations stop nowhere, and the exquisite problem of the artist is eternally but to draw, by a geometry of his own, the circle within which they shall happily *appear* to do so."[46] And James was a master of that kind of narrative drawing. Virginia Woolf and T. S. Eliot agreed that what one ultimately finds in James, especially in his late works, is not plot but a fabric of relations (though accessed through the point of view of an intelligent organizing mind, a focal nexus). One must look for a kind of figure, "not a plot, or a collection of characters, or a view of life, but something more abstract, more difficult to grasp, the weaving together of many themes into one theme, the making out of a design."[47] "The focus is a situation, a relation, an atmosphere, to which the characters pay tribute, but being allowed to give only what the writer wants."[48] And Georg Lukács, in his theory of the novel as the (anti-)epic of a world that has lost the simple givenness of national, communal, natural, and religious totalities, claims that modern literary narratives depend on the contingent and personal beginnings, middles, and ends of biographical lives to bring order to a world that has collapsed into fragments—as if every novel is a *Bildungsroman* by default, as perhaps classical Hollywood films too become, in miniature.[49]

In a work of narrative art, a network is a small world. Its limits are largely determined by "what the writer wants." We might first think of small worlds, by themselves, like tight clusters of close friends grouped around a single lunch table, cliquish and insular. These clusters express a series of strong social ties, connecting individuals in dense, homogeneous networks like friend groups and kinship units. Sociologist Mark Granovetter, in *The Strength of Weak Ties* (1973), famously articulates a vision of society structured by tight knots of strong ties, which are in turn connected to other such clusters by weak social ties (one can imagine slimmer, more fragile threads connecting individuals in different cliques). Granovetter's larger point is that we must pay close attention to the weak ties and what they do to understand how network society works. Duncan J. Watts, in a more recent popular sociology of "the connected age", explains:

> You only know who you know, and maybe *most* of the time, your friends know the same sort of people you do. But if just *one* of your friends is friends with just *one* other person who is friends with someone not like you at all, then a connecting path exists. You may not be able to use that path, you may not know it's there, and finding it may be difficult. But it *is* there. And when it comes to the propagation of ideas, influence, or even disease, that path can matter whether you know about it or not.[50]

Weak ties are lines of communication and transmission with the world at large. They are channels of new information and vectors of causal, if not always conscious, influence.

Network narratives, then, may be distinguished from their others by revising James's "exquisite problem" in a subtle way. If relations in reality stop nowhere, and the artist is the one who frames a circle in which they appear to, then the network artist is one who frames the circle (or rectangle) in which relations appear *not* to stop, though of course they must. That is, network narratives construct small worlds that give the impression of infinite expanse, with character relations proliferating endlessly beyond the frame outside our purview. Hence the opportunism of network story discourse: framed by a place or location (the Maison Vauquer boardinghouse in Balzac's *Père Goriot* or the La Colinière estate in Renoir's *La règle du jeu* or the Singaporean Housing Development Board (HDB) block in *12 Storeys*, hotels or bars or workplaces or hangout spots or large country houses where men and women gather on the eve of a fox hunt, or in more expanded geographical areas like a specific city or town or province); by a marked temporal span or holiday (like Christmas, New Year's, or Valentine's Day in recent mass market ensemble films like *Love Actually*); by a punctual event out of which radiates individual plotlines (car crashes or other chance meetings); by a concept that generates episodes or vignettes (love or death or grief, the decalogue of the Ten Commandments, *Thirteen Conversations About One Thing*, whatever that thing is); by a circulating object (the rifle in *Babel*, money in *Adventures of a 10-Mark Note* or Bresson's *L'Argent*); by a family or a self-defined friend group or posse (from Mann's *Buddenbrooks* to Márquez's *One Hundred Years of Solitude* to any number of biological or chosen families and their histories and struggles). And of course, in most cases network narratives combine two or more of these mechanisms: exploring love in Dublin (*Goldfish Memory*); a burst of noir complexity bounded in both space and time (*2 Days in the Valley*); a friend group struggling with the specter of adulthood together (*Things to Do Before You're 30*). The broad applicability of each network concept or conceit must be reined in by an a priori framework that will give the storyteller the motivation to use a small world as a stand-in for whichever thematic resonances the text generates. Films that depend most on thematic or tonal links between storylines rather than carefully interwoven plot threads work like bus topologies—semi-autonomous vignettes are strung together on a single main link, with slim overlaps between characters who at most serve as minor points of contact in other stories. *Things You Can Tell Just by Looking at Her* (dir. Rodrigo García, 2000) uses the bus form to connect women who share only their lacks; each story node presents another canary trapped in her individual cage, searching for the interrelation the film itself, unbeknownst to each, seeks to provide.

It is all a matter of degree. Network form is itself a nexus of various spectra, and novelists and filmmakers can always trade in detail for explanatory power and vice versa. So some network narratives chase totality as far it can go without abandoning story coherence altogether. They try, and perhaps inevitably fail, to map global systems. The drug trade (*Traffic*, 2000), the oil industry and its geopolitics (*Syriana*, 2005), the fast-food industry and its migratory patterns (*Fast Food Nation*, 2006)—each global network struggles its way into expression by attempting to name an adequate ensemble of representative characters and threading hierarchical systems into symbiotic ecologies. Into *story*. Neoliberal capitalism is one historical name for Jagoda's argument that network films "flourish in a cultural milieu characterized by an interest not only in network structure but also in dynamic processes of emergence: the creation of complex higher-level phenomena from interactions among lower-level components of a system."[51] He could be referring to biological emergence, or cognitive emergence, but by illustrating his claim with Stephen Gaghan's *Syriana*, Jagoda emphasizes the directness by which the film "engages with a transnational historical present" that conditions the making and distribution of most network films that have ever been made.

The transnational historical present, or what Fredric Jameson more directly calls late capitalism, is inherently difficult to narrate or describe. He references urban theorist

Kevin Lynch's *The Image of the City* (1960) as a starting point for conceiving contemporary (postmodern) geographical space as one "in which people are unable to map (in their minds) either their own positions or the urban totality in which they find themselves."[52] The "alienated city" becomes a miniature version of Jameson's account of national and global totalities. Cognitive mapping is an activity of "situational representation on the part of the individual subject to that vaster and properly unrepresentable totality which is the ensemble of society's structures as a whole." It is a way of knowing where one stands in a totality that cannot be directly (or mimetically) imaged. As such, for Jameson, it is always ideological in the Althusserian-Lacanian sense of representing "the imaginary relationship of individuals to their real conditions of existence."[53] Cognitive mapping is also always aesthetic, an act of imagination in perpetual motion, taking on more and more stress as global networks spread and intensify, as financialization spins into higher and higher levels of abstraction, as less and less of one's local, physiological purview determines the conditions of everyday life. And that holds wherever that life is lived, or wherever on earth one's internalized "You Are Here" arrow seems to point.

Like *Syriana* (of which more in a moment), Alejandro González Iñárritu's *Babel* (2006) is systematically global. The final film in the director's "Death Trilogy," *Babel* is a network film like its precedents, *Amores perros* (2000) and *21 Grams* (2003). The interlinks in the earlier films have single points of origin, car crashes in Mexico City in the former and an unspecified American city that appears to be Memphis in the latter. But *Babel*'s network spreads from Northern Africa to North America to the Asian Pacific, and its root structure is more rhizomatic, following from the circulation of international black-market trade, focused on a Winchester M70 rifle. As its title implies, globalism in the film is a condition pervaded by miscommunications and misunderstandings driven by language barriers and seemingly irreconcilable cultural differences. Vivien Silvey's reading of the film articulates a global village network ideology, doubling its optative tag to reinforce the sheer amount of supplication:

> If only, the film pleads, if only everyone in the world were able to understand each other then we would find solutions to these problems [racism, xenophobia, cultural ignorance] and heal the rifts that prolong pain and prejudice. The networks between these disparate characters afford opportunities for such healing, the chain of events begs to be uncovered and the points at which mistakes were made and misunderstood beg to find illumination. Through network society and communication, *Babel* argues, the world can work together to find peace.[54]

Babel's narrative form self-authorizes by pushing the empathic value of networked perception, the solution to the big problems it diagnoses already contained from the beginning in its form, at first latent and potential and, as it stitches together its global threads, eventually manifest and actual.

Syriana was inspired by former CIA handler Robert Baer's memoir *See No Evil* (2003). Its network is global, like *Babel*'s, shot on five continents, set in various locations in the United States, Europe, and Middle East, and loosely gathering nodes in an interconnected post-9/11 terrorist, intelligence, and military-industrial complex. The film's tagline, "Everything is connected," could not be more predictable. But the complex political-espionage-thriller storylines bank on otherwise unpredictable connections across scales and levels and domains in an international system that gathers competing forces like the corporate oil industry, the US Department of Justice, clandestine operatives, arms traffickers, displaced workers, terrorist cells, and all those waging the war against them. As Jagoda puts it, "the film's tight interconnectivity oscillates between ordered paranoia and the chaos of unpredictable events."[55] The terrorist network, in *Syriana*, is the unpredictable, distributed non-site of explosive emergence, of the shock of the real that shatters the world's business as usual. Confusion is a fundamental part of the film's aesthetic, from its hectic camera movement and microscopic shot lengths to its rapid dialogue pace.

One could also see the film's resistance to viewer processing as a symptom of cinema's *limitations* in narrating via global networks. Gaghan thought as much when making *Syriana*: "Five plot lines broke the camel's back.... If the stories all take place in the same geographical setting, it's easier to incorporate more strands. We shot over 200 locations on four continents with 100 speaking parts, and we found that we couldn't balance any more than four stories."[56] Since global network narratives demand parallel plots centered on characters in far-flung locations, there may in fact be a harder cap on the number of story threads one can coherently process, both for screenwriters and filmmakers, and for viewers. Charles Ramírez Berg claims that D. W. Griffith hit the limit at the very beginning of narrative cinema with his four stories told at great spatio-temporal distances in *Intolerance* (1916).[57] The more networks sprawl the more hyper-objective they become, their nodes everywhere and nowhere. When traditional cognitive maps fail to grasp totalities, narrative forms feel the tension. In films like *Syriana*, the necessary limitations of established narrative unities—time, space, action—produce network affect, the *feeling* of elsewheres and overdetermined causes that impinge on screened lifeworlds, and on the formal coherence of every present and presence.

Graphing Networks

If network narratives are provisional maps of unrepresentable social totalities, small worlds traced and embedded within large ones, their cartographical structures nevertheless differ from the more straightforwardly mathematical graphs that characterize twentieth-century scientific network theory. In the mid-1960s, Stanley Milgram, the social psychologist famous for his controversial experiments on obedience and authority, performed his so-called "small-world experiments" meant to test the average path length—the average number of chain links or steps on the shortest paths between node pairs—of social networks. He sent a letter to random individuals in Omaha, Nebraska and Wichita, Kansas with the aim of testing paths of association from those subjects to Milgram's friend in Boston. Recipients in the Midwest were informed of the Boston correspondent's identity and asked if they knew him personally. If they did, they could forward the letter directly to him. If, far more likely, they did not, they were asked to forward the letter to anyone they did know who would be more likely to know the target person in Boston (directions which would be repeated with each new recipient). At each potential stop along the way, pre-addressed postcards were sent to Milgram and his fellow researchers at Harvard, allowing them to track each path as it proceeded.

Not only did many of the letters make it to the target, but the average path length was—you guessed it—approximately six. Granted, Milgram's methods were legitimately critiqued on several grounds[58]; my aim here is not to validate the experiments' results but to place them in the context of network theory. Zooming out, they served as another link in the chain of network thinking, one that would lead to more experiments and more sophisticated social models.

Although their study was conducted before Milgram's and provided a conceptual foundation for the more famous small-world experiments, Ithiel de Sola Pool and Manfred Kochen's "Contacts and Influence" was published in 1978 in the inaugural issue of the aptly titled journal *Social Networks*. Pool and Kochen aimed to study the degree distribution of social networks, their overall structures or shapes, and to define the types of individuals within social networks and the relations between social influence and degree values. Certain individuals in any given social network serve as prolific connectors. To return to Milgram's experiment, a man known as "Mr. Jacobs" forwarded around two-thirds of the letters that successfully reached their target, and two men called "Mr. Brown" and "Mr. Jones" forwarded most of the rest.[59] These three men emerge as social network hubs, the main rail stations of the social world under observation.

Pool and Kochen appealed to the "random graph" studied a few decades earlier by Anatol Rapoport and developed into an influential model in graph theory by Paul Erdős and Alfréd Rényi (whose series of articles they co-authored on network formation were titanic achievements of synthesis, establishing the fundamental relationship between network complexity and randomness). Rapoport and Ray Solomonoff, in a 1951 study, ask readers to consider a graph with its nodes connected in a random fashion. The average number of nodes reachable in a network from another, randomly chosen node they call "weak connectivity." Weak connectivity can also be measured as the network's average component size, or the average quantity of nodes in any connected group that does not connect with a larger set. Rapoport and Solomonoff demonstrated how an increase in a network's average degree size (the ratio of links to nodes) eventually hits an inflection point where a group of disconnected nodes enter a state of connection, generating a "giant component," a component containing most of the graph's connected vertices. This happens quickly as one adds edges. Connectivity, which became a central concept of modern graph theory, measures the resilience of a network. Take a network of city streets. To simplify, imagine looking at a map of its layout from the perspective of a motorist. The streets themselves are links or edges. We can call intersections nodes of small degree, and well-located sites like major parks, municipal halls, or cultural centers (easy to get to, at the nexus of major boulevards) the city's hubs. In network parlance, some streets are undirected (two-ways, traversable from either direction, from intersection A to B or from B to A) while others are directed (one-ways, traversable in only one direction, from intersection C to D but not from D to C). As vehicles traverse the network, traffic congestion and gridlock, infrastructural breakdown, temporary closures, and even unexpected acts of political resistance and occupation can test its overall resilience, the city's capacity to withstand local connectivity failures. A network's resilience is its adaptability to crisis, its capacity to maintain flow when vertices go dark and the movement of information or activity between nodes must be redirected. Which requires high degrees of connectivity, of course—a large number of roads that provide options for turning off and taking efficient detours, relatively few dead ends and long oneways without intersections, and major thruways with enough lanes (capacity) for an increase in vehicle traffic above the daily average (higher node flow).

A system of streets with cars flowing through serves as a legitimate, practical example of graph theory's foundational perspective on how networks work. We can count a city's nodes and links, the degrees of its vertices, the relation between its order (number of nodes) and size (number of links), how centralized or distributed the city plan is (measurable by the range and deviation of hub degrees). And all this, translated into ordinary language, can tell us a lot about how well or poorly a city's streets have been designed and engineered. Some of this, of course, is a matter of urban aesthetics—whether one prefers a more centralized or distributed city depends on more than just traffic patterns. But even at the more foundational level of mathematical description there are concerns about the limitations of graph theoretical thinking for grasping what networks really are. Galloway and Thacker stress a few different points here, about what graph theory omits.

Graph theory might mislead us about networks in three big ways, Galloway and Thacker argue: on "the question of agency," by way of the theory's "diachronic blindness," and on "the question of internal complexity and topological incompatibility."[60] By the first they mean an assumption that nodes are active and agential, while the graph's edges are passive, mere relations of force set into motion by the nodes, like servants or handmaidens carrying their information. This has the effect of (incorrectly, Galloway and Thacker think) dividing "actor and action" in networks too neatly and privileging spatial models too eagerly. Indeed, referring to my previous example, street systems are particularly useful in explaining a graph theoretical approach to networks because they are not network metaphors, but active and explorable examples. So are other transportation systems. They are relatively easy models to grasp because, like the Seven Bridges of Königsberg, they are concretely spatial, if very large. The same goes for Milgram's social network experiments, because even though the thing being measured is abstract (social links are not literally laid out in space, nor do they have material bodies), paths between the network's nodes were articulated by geographical locations traversed by post, by vehicles and carriers bearing messages sent into circulation by the vertices (here, actual people). And although the network's Eulerian path need not be unidirectionally linear, there was still an implicit sense of spatial proximity paralleling nodal proximity. But what happens when we look beyond spatially arrayed, continuously traversable networks?

That brings us to the second problem, graph theory's "diachronic blindness." "Paradoxically," Galloway and Thacker write, "the geometrical basis (or bias) of the division between 'nodes' and 'edges' actually works against an understanding of networks as sets of relations existing in time."[61] Movement and flow are suggested by the network graph, especially in the case of directed links, but because of its synchronic bias—the network represented always exists as a slice of network time, as a single snapshot pulled out of its evolutionary lifespan—network geometry always betrays the underlying phenomena's tendency to change, resist stasis, and reorganize. Structural, synchronic discreteness is an impossibility, an artificial and misleading fiction. It is a feature of urban plans to change, for the infrastructure underlying a city's streets to need reinforcement and new features, for road networks to expand and adapt to new inputs or demands. And those are not accidental properties of networks but inherent ones, elided by the traditional graphs. Networks *emerge*, and while single graphs may imply emergence, they cannot present it. Network narratives are one of the means we have to present and experience emergence thematically.

Finally, Galloway and Thacker claim that graph theory fails to adequately represent incompatible topologies within networks, preferring to model alternative topologies separately rather than coexisting. A topology in this context refers to the shape or arrangement of a network's nodes, its physical description in terms of abstract spatial properties: the six most common are buses, rings, stars, trees, meshes, and hybrids. In keeping with their skepticism about any network having a fully stable geometric structure, Galloway and Thacker appeal to systems theory to define networks as "consist[ing] of aggregate interconnections of dissimilar subnetworks," topologies in the process of forming or deforming in tension with other subnetworks.[62] Categories of network topologies include meshes, stars, rings, buses, and trees. The Internet is a case in point, since it is usually described as a fully distributed mesh, as in peer-to-peer file sharing networks:

> But it is impossible to dissociate this technical topology from its motive, use, and regulation, which also make it a social topology of a different form (file-sharing communities), an economic topology with a still different form (distribution of commodities), and even a legal one (digital copyright). All of these networks coexist, and sometimes conflict with each other, as the controversy surrounding file sharing has shown.[63]

The biggest insight of Galloway and Thacker's critique of network theories attempting faithful translations of graph theory is that they tend to diminish network dynamics, the principle that ultimately defines networks in the first place and in the last instance. No network's components, degree ratios, agential relationships, and topologies are fixed for all time (or even for very long), and our descriptions and analyses must account for (and should even privilege, on their view) the dimension of network activity.

The Big Web

In 1998, two doctoral students in computer science at Stanford published a paper titled "The Anatomy of a Large-Scale Hypertextual Web Search Engine." Authors Sergey Brin and Lawrence Page define the web as "a vast collection of completely uncontrolled heterogeneous documents" that "vary significantly in language, format, and style" and present magnitudinous differences in "size, quality, popularity, and trustworthiness."[64] Though not infinite, the web was a Borgesian Library of Babel without a good catalog or a system of classification numbers to track specific texts down. Automated search engines and "human maintained indices" like Yahoo! existed, but the former's keyword-based process struggled with the quality of matches and the latter were limited by their subjective natures—slow to develop, expensive to maintain, and limited in total topic coverage.[65] The need for advertising revenue only added to the problems, as search engine results were routinely and systematically manipulated to direct click flow to monetized pages.

Brin and Page named the solution Google (a variant of googol, or ten raised to the power of one hundred). Which gives you a sense of their ambition and confidence in the amount of web information their engine would be able to process. Their first algorithm, PageRank, improved on extant systems by treating the web *as a web*, that is, as a network of relevance relations and links rather than a box with a very large number of individual pages. Links can be thought of like up votes vouching for the value of another page. To personify it: every link, in other words, is akin to someone sticking up for a friend, telling everyone else that he's cool and can be part of the group. Or like scholars citing each other, thereby recursively increasing each other's authority. Inevitably there are the loser pages, unlinked and off on their own; they fall way down on Google's search results. John Durham Peters puts it nicely: "Google reads the web as the map of itself. The mathematics of expander graphs applied to the web sees it as something like rainfall on a landscape: the aim is not to know every square inch of soil but to figure out topography from the water flows."[66] The water, or the informational content, is inferred "from their location in networks" rather than picked out by scanning for exact terminology.

The Internet in general, and the question of how best to search and map its perpetually growing web, changed network theory. Albert-László Barabási, physicist and network scientist, articulates the shift as a deeper awareness of the ubiquity of *scale-free networks* rather than the random networks pushed by the Erdős-Rényi model. Whereas the degree distribution of a random network follows a bell curve—so that most of its nodes have the same mean number of links, and nodes with very few or very many links mostly do not exist—a scale-free network's distribution follows a power law. A power law degree distribution requires that most nodes have very few links, with the network as a whole secured by a very small number of extremely well-connected hubs. An example of the former is the US federal highway network; the air traffic network, on the other hand, is scale free.[67]

The World Wide Web is an even better illustration. As of 2024 it is estimated to contain over five billion pages. When we surf the web, we are following a hyper-small path through an immense network of pages. Only when we zoom out to consider its global network topology do we understand how far the web is from randomness. Starting from a random page, a minority of the total web is accessible via surfing (by following links). A "central core" of websites is made up of all major pages accessible to each other along a path of links. But there are equally large "continents" of the web network made up of pages that contain paths either into that central core (you can get to the central core by following links from one of its pages) or out of it (you can start in the central core and follow links to it). You cannot follow those "in" or "out" paths in reverse.[68] A fourth continent, made up of "islands" and "tendrils," are isolated from the central core and contain interconnected pages that cannot reach the web's core *and* are unreachable from it. Barabási and his team took an important lesson from this uneven topological structure: "As long as [a network's] links remain directed," as long as they point to each other in one rather than both directions, as many web links do, "homogenization will never occur."[69] The fragmented continental structure we see in the World Wide Web is not unique to it, but forms in any directed network.

So even though the Internet is often used as an example of utopian freedom, of open access to all information, of liberatory horizontality that puts all hierarchical power under siege as it grows, it might better be seen as the ultimate case in point for the new power arrangements immanent to scale-free networks. Barabási finds power laws everywhere, from the global economic system to the workings of a single biological cell. It is as if, pushed by the Internet and the exponentially growing web to see hubs everywhere and in everything, network theory as Barabási practices it—burying and eulogizing Erdős and Rényi's random networks—naturalizes inequality of power and influence as the necessary result of growth in any domain. Scale-free networks are not, however, the origin of life itself: "Nature normally hates power laws."[70] Systems follow bell curve distributions *until forced to undergo a phase transition*, an insight that joins network theory to systems theory. For our purposes we need only recognize that transitions from disorder to order, randomness into structure—whether we are talking about water freezing into ice or the stratification of income levels into a top-heavy distribution symptomatic of capitalism—follow power laws ("nature's unmistakable sign that chaos is departing in favor of order"). The celebrated self-organization of real networks as they grow not only doesn't guarantee radical equality; it continuously works against it. The question is whether power laws are irrevocably ingrained in nature's transitional processes, or whether nature contains the tools (human social activity? narrative modes?) to control the protocols native to scale-free networks.

Graphing Narratives

So the biggest and most powerful networks we observe are scale-free, tending over time to organize around a small number of large hubs. But that does not guarantee anything about the network form of any narrative text, which is not completely constrained by the manner in which real networks self-organize. If Barabási's critique of Erdős and Rényi's model depends on substituting networks as active processes for misleadingly static diagrams, we might then ask where narrative texts fit the picture. Does it follow that graphing network narratives is a fool's errand? Not everyone thinks so. "A network is made of vertices and edges; a plot, of characters and actions: characters will be the vertices of the network, interactions the edges, and here is what the *Hamlet* network looks like," according to Moretti.[71] Right away, Moretti acknowledges that his graph is far from an objectively correct network presentation of Shakespeare's tragedy. To graph a narrative you code its data, which involves choosing how to pin its elements down into categories. What, for instance, is an interaction between two characters? Moretti links them if "some words have passed between them." James Stiller, Daniel Nettle, and Robin I. M. Dunbar also treat Shakespearean characters as vertices in their attempt to articulate a play's network structure, but take a different approach to linking them, "deeming two characters to be linked if there was at least one time slice of the play in which both were present (that is, if two characters spoke to each other *or were in each other's presence*, then they have a link)."[72] Moretti notes that the difference in these two approaches, which are still only two of many possible ways of coding character interaction, is revealed by the difference in densities of resulting network graphs ("My network uses explicit connections, theirs adds implicit ones, and is obviously denser, because it has all my edges plus some"[73]). What about actions one character takes for or against another at a spatio-temporal distance of at least one scene? What about one character speaking about another behind their back? Does an appearance in a dream count as an interaction? What one counts as in or out drives the density of the network representation. The alternatives Moretti discusses are literary network representations in their infancy, leaving much to be desired. Neither the nodes nor the links are weighted; the graphs tell us that two characters interact, but not how significant those interactions are (how many lines long or how many times they take place, to take two easily countable variables). And none of the edges show direction; it seems particularly relevant in a drama to be able to visualize the difference between a one-way or two-way interaction, whether specific links entail balanced dialogue, unbalanced dialogue, or one-way address.

As (some) scholars in the humanities have become more sophisticated programmers and quantitative analysts, they have produced more complicated programs for mapping texts as networks. Because this is a book without a digital component, I will only briefly mention one way this can be done (and has been done) to represent the active *creation* of a character network through the forward movement of narrative. After all, since all narratives evolve, change, and develop before they end, their underlying network structures change too. Even following Moretti's simple method, one could diagram *Hamlet*'s character network anew with every new link added over the course of the play, beginning with Barnardo and Francisco only and progressively adding nodes as each new character is introduced (and links as each extant character interacts with someone new, and maybe additional weight as they interact again, and so on). And one could, instead of putting all these different diagrams together like a flipbook, develop a digital program that shows the network evolving with each scene. Without understanding these sorts of network dynamics, we do not fully understand networks, whether in textual form or otherwise. As they grow and complexify, old nodes that were initially unconnected develop new internal links, and some links disappear (whereas Moretti's simplest

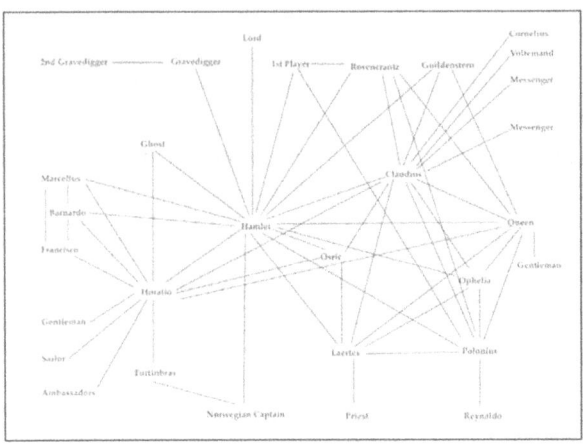

FIGURE 1 *Moretti's* Hamlet *network. Reproduced with the permission of Franco Moretti.*

diagram retains every interaction that happens over the course of the play, we could also represent at every moment characters growing apart, so that links articulate the *rate* at which they interact, or even characters dying, their nodes disappearing from the diagram altogether). This may be easier to envision in an ever-evolving network diagram of the World Wide Web, where links between two pages often disappear and therefore sever their direct edges, or are added, or are replaced by links to other pages. Considered as models of narrative development, networks do not simply sit, atemporally, behind texts or works; they rewire themselves as they go.

But back to the simpler map we have here. *Hamlet* is one of the least networked of Shakespeare's plays, in the sense of character distribution. And yet it can be shown to have or be a network too, no matter how central a presence Prince Hamlet is, no matter how much physical and verbal space he takes up. Which does not mean *Hamlet* is a network play in any useful definition of the term, whereby "network play" we mean something that distinguishes it from another dramatic type or form. Really, the question Moretti's diagrammatic analysis poses is: if "network theory could offer a way to quantify plot," and if every multi-character plot can be quantified as a network, what narrative text *isn't* a network?[74] Moretti's choice of *Hamlet* (I am speculating) relies on the centrality of Hamlet as a character, the fact that at any given moment, as audience, we are quite likely to be seeing and hearing him speak, to himself or to others, while most other characters are (statistically) unlikely to be there. Moretti's network diagrams, just like the graphs, maps, and trees he produces elsewhere, make temporal forms (narratives proceeding in time) spatial, the diachronic made synchronic:

> What do we gain, by turning time into space? First of all, this: when we watch a play, we are always in the present: what is on stage, is; and then it disappears. Here, nothing ever disappears. What is done, cannot be undone. Once the Ghost shows up at Elsinore things change forever, whether he is on scene or not, because he is never not there in the network. The past becomes past, yes, but it never disappears from our perception of the plot.[75]

Network models, if sufficiently but accurately inclusive, make every relevant connection visible. Then what makes *Hamlet* not count as a network play, at least as I am using the modifier "network" to group narrative works? Because in reading or viewing *Hamlet*, sans quantitative analysis, we are not particularly goaded by its narrative form to think of its diegetic space *as* a network, *as* a spatial whole. In a way, network mapping shows this. There are (narrative) *regions* of the play that are densely networked, though in that region Hamlet is just one of several characters clustering around Claudius. Upon reflection, the biggest (self-acknowledged) problem with Moretti's diagram, that it does not weight character nodes by lines or time on stage, can help us understand why the dense, highly connected cluster around Claudius does not represent the way readers and viewers imagine the society in and around Elsinore. If we took this densely networked region alone, abstracted from the rest of the play's character system, Hamlet could disappear from the stage without much of an effect on the relationships between Claudius, Gertrude, Polonius, Ophelia, and Laertes. We know this to be a misreading of the play, even if it is an accurate statement about the structure of Claudius's court. Because without Hamlet—as Moretti's diagram shows—there would be only the most tenuous link, through the helper Horatio, between the characters clustering around Claudius and the foundation for the entire play's complex (anti-)revenge plot: the Ghost of Hamlet's father.

The boundaries between network and non-network narratives are fuzzy, but not unlocatable. The boundaries are also multiple, not a single, countable threshold of any kind. Every narrative may be networkable, in other words, but a far smaller number distinguish their structure and form in a way that goads readers and viewers to *recognize* its story or discourse as a network. Network narratives insist on networking, put their money into it, at the expense of other formal processes. Another way of putting it is that although just about every narrative discourse networks its corresponding story world to an extent, what we call network narratives usually provide more of a random network than a scale-free one—they *push against* social tendencies to establish power laws, which takes narrational effort—in that their nodes become *characteristic*, flaunting a (relative, never absolute) democracy of links against the traditional winner-takes-all discourse of protagonist-driven narratives. Some network films bear the stress of their own anti-hierarchical form more than others. Jonathan Demme's *Handle with Care* (originally released 1977 as *Citizens Band*) is another one of those films directly influenced by Altman; it could have been tagged as "*Nashville* on the airwaves." Its opening sequence overlaps voices in the night, a Nebraska *sinfonia*, all reaching out over channels on the Citizens Band (CB) frequency range, crossing and blending. Instead of seeing their sources first we see the radio network's hardware—antennae, wires, boxes, circuit boards, and dials. We hear the enveloping noise of the system, its static, eating at every utterance like a parasite. "Is there something wrong with my modulation? I just don't want to lose my modulation." "You don't sound too good. I mean, not your radio but your voice." "How do you know if anyone's listening?" "There are a lot of voices out there, but yours is different. I like it." "Hello?" Whether you see people or not—perhaps especially when you don't—they are out there, like frequencies traversing the space of a nocturnal dream, searching for a response to validate their transmission, which is the same thing as their existence.

The noise, though, is also the problem. The radio band is overcrowded; illegal stations clutter the airwaves and Emergency Channel 9 is overtaken by pranksters. Radio Emergency Associated Communication Teams (REACT) volunteer Spider (Paul Le Mat) aims to centralize the network. And his effort to silence the band's pirates, including a neo-Nazi and a child who reads pornographic stories on the air, reveals the formal struggle at the heart of all network forms, including the very film nesting his DIY hero's journey at its nodal center. The hero, in any narrative, exists as such only at the expense of those minor characters who would hijack his story if they could. Pirates always circle, out for blood or booty. The arena in which characters compete for available narrative bandwidth is, as Alex Woloch calls it in a wonderful study of the novel, "character space."[76] The character space of any narrative text is finite; there is only so much pie to go around, though everyone wants seconds. Protagonists get unfairly large portions, while minor characters are often left with crumbs. *Handle with Care* self-consciously networks character space by making its plot conflicts share the form of a meta-conflict in the narration. There is plot and meta-plot, in other words. In the former, Spider navigates a crowded field of CB radio users vying for space on the network, with formally similar side plots proliferating, like love contests between Spider and his brother over cheerleading coach Pam/Electra, and trucker Chrome Angel's reckoning with the discovery by his two wives that the other exists and that he has been splitting his time between two families (and, likely, many other women). Every storyline involves a competition for mini-protagonist status, against the field of rivals. Like nodes competing for links, the competition—as a matter of narrative discourse, not story—is one of *fitness*, a term used to describe the relative intra-network propensity to acquire new edges. In the larger meta-plot, the film as a whole can be seen as a character space, where a network of networks (storylines, smaller domains where characters compete) produces a protagonist—Spider—who emerges in relief, against all others. He is fit to be a hero, of sorts, but he has to earn it over the course of the film. And like in many network narratives, the pool of applicants is filled with folks more ordinary in their qualifications than the paladins and celebutantes of yesteryear.

If every narrative film has a character space and a "character system" through which shares of narrative influence are distributed, then we might call some films networks because of the intentional equality of character power in their distributions. Not every film, in other words, has a clear protagonist, or a protagonist at all, though we can imagine every character in a network film vying for our attention, implicitly demanding that we look and listen to them every time they enter a scene. Horatio does not steal any of Hamlet's scenes, but Mercutio steals Romeo's and maybe dies early in that play because of it. In *Handle with Care*, all the minor characters who have been exiled from the main stream of the narrative, their transmission cables cut, in order to swell the space of the protagonist's band and his parallel mission as would-be romantic hero, return in the film's final sequence to help search for Spider's lost father (a nostalgic CB user who would prefer to live on the airwaves as his old avatar, Papa Thermodyne, than trouble with his flesh and blood children and their pets). There are many voices out there, Electra tells Spider in the end, but she likes his best. The early modern philosopher Gottfried Wilhelm Leibniz famously wrote about standing by the ocean, listening to its chaotic mixture of crashes and swirls, thinking that its noise exists only for finite beings like him and not for God, whose omniscience brooks no confusion. God would hear every sound distinctly. On the airwaves, though, there is always noise. We strain to hear the one voice that truly hails us. Network films strive for omniscience but court its failure; characters who self-consciously recognize themselves as nodes in a network strive for centrality but never solve the problem of the existence of other people. Even though network form always regulates randomness into some principle(s) of totality—just the way Spider fights the inexorable processes of informational entropy, regulates the deregulated band, and progressively assumes character centrality—there remains a counterpressure toward celebrating (and continually insisting upon) the open, even chaotic relationality of modern life. In the end, it just comes down to which voice you happen to like best. Liberal pluralism as narrative form.

Everything Is Everything(?)

The world's most famous network theorist, the late Bruno Latour, offers an ambitious theoretical pluralism that aims to take the sociology of networks beyond the human domain. In *The Pasteurization of France* (1993), Latour tells the story of his emergence as the ultimate theoretical leveler: "At the end of the winter of 1972, on the road from Dijon to Gray, I was forced to stop, brought to my senses after an overdose of reductionism."[77] His roadside mantra went, "Nothing can be reduced to anything else, nothing can be deduced from anything else, everything may be allied to everything else. This was like an exorcism that defeated demons one by one."[78] Horizons opened, clouds cleared, and devils evaporated.

One may be excused for assuming the story is but a wink at Pauline or Augustine conversion crises; Latour's countryman Rousseau told of a strikingly similar experience on the road from Paris to Vincennes. Cheeky allusion or no, Graham

Harman writes that "[a]n entire philosophy is foreshadowed in this anecdote."[79] If an entire philosophy is foregrounded by Latour's existential exorcism, so is an intellectual lineage backgrounded. My aim is not to trace that genealogy (post-Durkheim) in intense detail but to sketch its basic lineaments as we look at contemporary uses of the network concept in theory. Latour's anecdote, his experience of purifying clarity on the road to French Damascus, first suggests that network theory as he develops it depends on flattening phenomena into a metaphysical democratic body, eliminating hierarchies that have been said to inhere among objects and concepts until everything answers to everything else and nothing reduces into anything else. Nothing disappears; nothing is colonized; everything appears; everything participates. Easier said than to really believe or perceive.

The Actor-Network Theory (ANT) associated most closely with Latour, and developed in the early 1980s alongside Michel Callon, Madeleine Akrich, and John Law, attempts a transformation from a "sociology of the social" to a "sociology of associations."[80] The former "traditional" path assumes a fixed, stable social order that grounds the possibilities and potentialities of its members. The latter begins with associations, tracks them across time, while bracketing from consideration any encompassing, underlying structure. Latour, perhaps surprisingly, enlists a conservative heroine as the spokesperson for this sociology of associations:

> It claims that there is nothing specific to social order; that there is no social dimension of any sort, no "social context," no distinct domain of reality to which the label "social" or "society'"could be attributed; that no "social force" is available to "explain" the residual features other domains cannot account for; that members know very well what they are doing even if they don't articulate it to the satisfaction of the observers; that actors are never embedded in a social context and so are always much more than "mere informants" . . . and that "society," far from

being the context "in which" everything is framed, should rather be construed as one of the many connecting elements circulating inside tiny conduits. With some provocation, this second school of thought could use as its slogan what Mrs. Thatcher famously exclaimed (but for very different reasons!): "There is no such a thing as a society."[81]

Latour reprints and disseminates Thatcher's "There is no such thing as a society" (guided by "very different reasons") as an anti-ontological slogan, rallying the exorcists to purify sociology of any substantive, "wooden" or "steely," definition of society as the bedrock domain of human-centric reality.[82] And the idea that there is "no social force'" available as the last resource of explanation for empirically observed patterns of human relations, behavior, and organizational structures does challenge a fundamental assumption of "traditional" sociology and anthropology.

Latour does not want to bring sociology back in line with the social contract tradition Durkheim critiqued. He is not saying: there is no society, only individuals. He seeks a third way, shimmying through the narrow pass between classically liberal individualism and newly liberal assumptions that society is a "stabilized state of affairs, a bundle of ties" that emits a magnetic force determining specific structures ("posit[ing] the existence of a specific sort of phenomenon called 'society,' 'social order,' 'social practice,' 'social dimension,' or 'social structure'").[83] Society, in other words, conceived as a thing, an entity, governed by laws just as fixed as nature's (laws that produce social rather than natural facts). Christopher Herbert tracks the permutations of this idea through the nineteenth century and into Durkheim's sociological method, through E. B. Tylor's *Primitive Culture* (1871) and the work of Spencer, Franz Boas, Ruth Benedict, Bronislaw Malinowski, Marcel Mauss, Claude Lévi-Strauss, and several other culture theorists, as the concept of the "complex whole," the "presumption that that [the] array of disparate-seeming elements of social life composes a significant *whole*, each factor of which is in some sense a corollary of, consubstantial with, implied by, immanent in, all the others."[84] Society, according to this picture, *is* the unobservable wholeness that causes or creates the customs, beliefs, and values held in common by a human collective.

One name for the force that caulks the gaps in sociocultural wholes, in the Durkheim-Mauss-Lévi-Strauss line of thinking, is *mana*. A Polynesian and Melanesian term, mana is a sacred, supernatural, impersonal force that invests totems, sites, speakers, and other entities with efficacious social power. William Mazzarella, in a recent book on "the mana of mass society," begins his account of the concept with Durkheim's description of "a certain rush of energy," constitutive of any society, that never "fails to come to us from outside ourselves" at every moment.[85] In Mauss's theory of the gift, mana is what invests an object with the ritual power to circulate in an exchange system based on more than atomistic acts of buying and selling commodities. Modern anthropology tried to rid itself of such a "primitive" notion, but it returns like the undead, often by other names, a residual spiritualism that animates group consciousness like a cocktail shot into the venae cavae of collective life. Lévi-Strauss would demystify mana, to be sure, conceiving it less as intrinsically sacred than as an empty, floating signifier, something with no natural value but which has the capacity (*because* of its emptiness) to assume many social meanings. Thus, its "force" as a binding social power expresses any and every society's *failure* to completely cohere, its unerasable contradictions. Social networks, whether conceived as primitive kinship structures, modern civil societies, or postmodern mass culture, are then thought to work through the circulation of empty signifiers. Powerfully meaningless, mana names whatever signs or rituals quilt the network's complex meshwork. Either excessive or empty, transcendent or a negation, it is what lends efficacy to a structure while pointing out the groundlessness of that structure.

Mazzarella, borrowing a concept from Lacanian psychoanalysis, calls mana "extimate," both external to social subjects and yet somehow also intimate, "that which we experience, ambivalently, as part of the world that confronts us and yet at the same time as something that is palpably, intensely, at the very core of our sense of ourselves."[86] But actor-network theory does not tolerate a concept like mana. For Latour, social formation is an endless process without any underlying agent or force generating the order or associations we observe and name. Not only is there a contradiction between the methodological empiricisms of modern anthropology and sociology ("just the facts, ma'am," as the great sociologist Joe Friday always says) and the guiding assumption of social wholes taken on board without ever being glimpsed. There is also the danger of endless circularity—the "specific sort of phenomenon called 'society'" sets the boundaries of what is possible within its parameters, and social facts, by virtue of falling within those parameters, make up the observable data for retroactively articulating what the society is. Actor-network theory's explicit attempt to break and discard this circle reveals how network theory proper emerges when a dominantly held cause like "society" or a metaphysical concept like the anthropological-sociological "social force," hard to experience or even explain, is rejected as the indispensable center of a web of sub-causes. When, that is, an invisible but stabilizing cause of a set or group is replaced by a distributed and continually forming process. When an autopoietic system is punctured in some way, its equilibrium form opened to further expansion.

But even listing these "moments" in the emergence of network theory reveals a potential problem: there may be a subtle rhetorical slippage between the theory and the theory's object, between the theory of networks and networks themselves. For Latour, this problem is supposed to be his theory's strength. Actor-network theory participates in forming the networks its practitioners write about, in reinforcing links between the actors it names. Traditional sociologists, Latour writes, "would much prefer to be like 'hard' scientists and try to understand the existence of a given phenomenon, refusing to consider the written account and relying instead on direct contact with the thing at hand via the transparent medium of a clear and unambiguous technical idiom."[87] Even more starkly: "good sociology has to be well written; if not, the social doesn't appear through it." So what is it about network theory or sociology, when written the way Latour likes it, that makes the social appear? Since Latour already rejects the "social force" as a stable and substantive entity forming any given social structure, the groups and agents his "sociology of associations" describes are not static or stable, nor do they precede and succeed the writing of their accounts. Actor-network theory is a process of tracing "ties" between "actors," the way social actors transform one another by translating one another, and articulating these mediations in an endless process of forming associations and recording them in writing.

To form and record at the same time means not taking the content of relations and associations for granted, not importing the set of actors and agents proper to the category in question—like society—ahead of representing or writing about it. For a theorist this entails a dizzying amount of freedom in the possible objects of attention, coupled with a demand for intense vigilance in maintaining a high level of empirical openness to new formations and deformations in the constructed network. ANT aims to block deductive recourse to forces or principles higher, deeper, or more foundational than the elements being observed, described, or related. If "network" is a proper term for what ANT posits and describes, it is always perceived as conceptually flat, with none of its nodes fundamentally higher or deeper (ontologically) than any other.

The most challenging aspect of Latour's ANT, at least for any attempt to ground it in network theory more broadly, is that actual networks are not privileged examples of the theory. "Network is a concept, not a thing out there," Latour writes. "It is a tool to help describe something and not what is being described."[88] So ANT is less a theory about the world than an activity that pokes around in it. Networks as Latour thinks them are not labyrinths that merely exist, are not even things that take on a net-like form, but the results of *translation,* an activity that "*creates* mixtures between entirely new types of beings, hybrids of nature and culture."[89] Networks are assemblages of *actors* or *actants* that translate, recruit, or incorporate other actors. When you list possible actor/actants, the more eclectic the catalog, the better: water molecules, sitcoms, exponents, high schools, Ferraris, cold fronts. The Latourian hodgepodge catalog trades on the assumption that these actors are fundamentally different, *different sorts of things*, only to level them by placing them in syntactic parallel, flattening intuited differences (of material, of scale, of abstraction). Ontologically, in the level of reality each partakes in, they are equivalent. "An atom is no more real than Deutsche Bank or the 1976 Winter Olympics," Harman explains, "even if one is likely to endure much longer than the others."[90] No actant reduces to any other, even though they do translate each other. And human beings, even in so-called social networks, are never the only nodes, are never even necessarily the primary ones. Yet it takes writing, a translative activity of non-intuitive assemblage, to see how this is so.

One of ANT's most important concepts, Latour says he uses translation "to mean displacement, drift, invention, mediation, the creation of a link that did not exist before and that to some degree modifies two elements or agents."[91] Every node in a network, every actant, includes its links, its relationships with other actants—there is no hard, dark, untouchable substance beneath its qualities and its relations (there is no unbreachable boundary between its interior and exterior). Links, in Latour's account of networks, *are* translations, since everything we could possibly identify as a node "demand[s] its share of reality," as Harman puts it.[92] And that reality is a nothing more nor less than an ongoing process of linkage, actions "not done under the full control of consciousness" but "as a node, a knot, and a conglomerate of many surprising sets of agencies that have to be slowly disentangled," knotted and unknotted catalogs of surprising assemblages or hybrids.[93] Though he pushes an immanent ontology where no actor sits inherently, hierarchically above any other in its share of reality, Latour does suggest a network ontology of degrees of existence: "The more attachments [an actor] has, the more it exists. And the more mediators there are the better."[94] The bigger the node we can draw, the more of existence we can perceive. This prescription, I hazard, could easily serve as the justification for network narratives and their wide but flat, horizontal, and connection-driven narrational forms: the more relations the better, because with each additional link more reality (even when fictional) appears.

Latour's concern is that we often shield reality from our theories about it by insisting mistakenly on systematic purification. To the guy who wrote *We Have Never Been Modern,* the contemporary crisis we face when we look at the world and its media representations is nothing short of the crisis of modernity *tout court.* When he says that "we have never been modern," Latour means primarily to recognize that living modernity is something altogether different, more complicated and less conceptually pure, than the theoretical apparatus academic intellectuals use to describe it. Threatening objects—like the hole in the ozone layer, the AIDS virus, or nuclear energy (all hybrids, or what Timothy Morton would call "hyper-objects")—oscillate between the categories of the social and natural. One cannot exhaust the characteristics of hybrids, both objective and discursive nodes at the vertices of sprawling networks, by appealing only to scientific-material or political-discursive explanations: "[Boyle's air pump, Pasteur's microbes, Archimedes' pulleys] possess miraculous properties because they are at one and the same time both social and asocial, producers of natures and constructors of subjects."[95] Latour's distinction between systems and networks is significant here: "More supple than the notion of system, more historical than the notion of structure, more empirical than the notion of complexity, the idea of network is the Ariadne's thread of [the] interwoven stories" told by interdisciplinary actors (like him) whose discourses cross the false boundary between nature and culture.[96] The key is the focus on the thread itself rather than the posited substance or substrate of the connections between objects. Translation, the actor-network alternative to purification, occurs when one traces the production of hybrids while bracketing the question of their rootedness in the natural, political, or social. Systems, on the other hand, presuppose foundations, and assume some objects or forces to be more real, complex, or even simply more interesting than all others (a vulgar Marxian analysis of base-superstructure relations is problematic for Latour because it posits economic forces as ontologically and causally primary to social products). For Latour, system thinking involves the influx of idealism into materialism, and betrays the flat, concrete, and immanent ontology of networks.

As a constructivist concept, translation essentially replaces the (intentional) act or action, and the network of translations replaces the traditional sociological ideal of "local, face-to-face, naked, unequipped, and dynamic interactions" which congeal thanks to "a sort of specific force that is supposed to explain why those same temporary face-to-face interactions could become far-reaching and durable."[97] The "sort of specific" gives Latour's game away; he emphasizes that any appeal to a social force as the glue causing or reinforcing human actions is "conspiracy theory, not social theory."[98] What does society look like without social glue? For Latour, and ANT generally, the difference between society at large (its macro scale) and individuals caught within it (its microbes) disappears, which dissolves the need to posit social forces connecting more plastic individual members to larger stable structures. In other words, society is topologically flat. Tracing the relationships between actors in a network, Latour thinks that you never jump scales from one network surface to another "higher" or "lower." As David J. Krieger and Andréa Belliger put it in their study of ANT and new media, "the result of sociological explanation [according to Latourian ANT] is not the description of macro structures, of determining mechanisms behind the backs of individuals, but an ever more detailed and individualized description of actors and the associations that arise from their activities of translating and enrolling."[99] The more you describe, the more you see actors (often non-human) rather than structures, and the associations appear as moving, shifting networks—some big, some small, some momentary, some sturdy.

Difficult questions certainly arise. I can only focus on one here. But it is a central problem for thinking about theories of network narrative. When Latour uses words like "agent" or "actor," he does not mean what ordinary language would suggest he means. Actor-network theory arguably begins with the perversion of traditional (and traditionally metaphysical) definitions of agency. Action, for Latour, does not require an attributable intention. And agency is motiveless action. As a way of escaping metaphysical Cartesian subject-object dualities, his theory of action has salutary effects, and it offers posthumanists shots at the biggest prizes in the game booth. Flight from the illest intellectual effects of anthropocentrism and Eurocentrism, for one, and a post-Enlightenment view of nature with all the social and political benefits that might entail. But do those ends justify attributing agency to all manner of objects, concepts, and assemblages? Does agency not imply intention? Alf Hornborg claims, quite reasonably, that attributing "agency, purposes, or intentions to non-living objects is tantamount to fetishism."[100] By flattening the conceptual relationship between agency and cause, actor-network theory risks flattening other substantive categories in its wake, like purpose, intentionality, consciousness, and subjectivity. We may accept, as Hornborg does, that all of these internalizations are "products of their external relations" and "shaped by and extended through ... engagement with other entities, both living and non-living," animate and inanimate, material and conceptual. In other words, as distributed and networked through and through. But that may not necessarily require that we give up all useful distinctions between agency and causal consequence. In fact, our ability to theorize network form—and use it as an aesthetic or narrative category—depends on our ability to make distinctions between agents and consequential non-agents, a difference necessary to the continued relevance of *character*.

Can an object be a character? Some literary critics say yes, doggedly. Bill Brown's "thing theory" is one kind of affirmation. He looks to literature that asks, less theoretically than narratively, "why and how we use objects to make meaning, to make or re-make ourselves, to organize our anxieties and affections, to sublimate our fears and shape our fantasies."[101] The poetics of attachment to material objects, the aesthetic logic of *thingification*, not only renders objects luminous, to Brown, but invests them with something like interiority, subjectivity, character. Is this mystification? No, at least not the same kind as the commodity fetish that structures the capitalist horizon of our object-world, Brown claims. He makes a distinction between the aesthetic fascination with objects revealed by thing theory and the "metaphysical subtleties and theological niceties" Marx attributes to the fetish of the commodity form.[102] In Brown's reading of Mark Twain's *The Prince and the Pauper*, the king's seal takes on parallax meanings—is it an object that signifies kingship and thereby grants authority on a particular individual, or is it just a nutcracker? The recognition and use of a physical object not only gives it meaning, makes it a thing—apart from its exchange-value as a commodity—but the object-as-thing also makes the subject who uses it, makes them a prince or a pauper, depending.[103] Thingliness, then, can be said to name the process of human-object networking, its two-way production of social meaning. Latour is just a footnote here. But ANT is the theoretical medium through which thing theory and its characterological interpretations flow.

The actor-network obsession with non-human, even inanimate agents may ultimately be a result of its drive to conceive networks as ceaselessly forming and de-forming. Agency must, for Latour, be reconceptualized in a way that includes and integrates any tie or mediator, the smallest micro-units that translate meaning between actors to whom we traditionally attribute purpose and intention. Whether this breaks the conceptual meaning of agency I leave to others for now. But Harman thoughtfully articulates the larger paradox of Latourian thinking: if actors are "defined entirely by their relations and alliances" and nothing more, they must be "perpetually perishing, since they cannot survive even the tiniest change in their properties."[104] If actors are defined solely by their relations, then, "*precisely for this reason* they are cut off in their own relational microcosms, which endure only for an instant before the actor is replaced by a similar actor."[105] Networks of connections start to seem like a collection of disconnections, since there are no nodes that remain what they are across the timespan of their established relation with others. Hence Latour's claim that "ANT is a method, and mostly a negative one at that; it says nothing about the *shape* of what is being described with it," nothing about a network's form.[106] If the network established by a description is formless and evanescent, anything with the appearance of network form is less interesting to Latour than something that does not.[107] The alternative to ANT is what I have called network formalism. Unlike actor-network theory, it may offer real tools for interpretive criticism, which depends on drawing some minimal boundary around the network or holding some level of consistency across time. Networking may be a ceaseless activity of translation and change, but if it is to be conceptually relevant to an interpretive community—like, say, film critics and historians—we must be able to name its features, to occasionally think of it as a descriptive noun.

Between Noun and Verb

How, then, do we represent, diagram, map, or *film* networks to show off their temporal dynamics? There are important differences between the spatial forms of network visualizations (whether static or evolving) and the temporal unfoldings of narratives in which networks are sensed, felt, or encountered at the edges of character, reader, or narratorial consciousness. Consider first Mark Lombardi's network drawings, conceptual artworks designed to reveal political histories of global financial flow through the media of conglomerates. They are visual, primarily spatialized narratives in diagrammatic network form. Lombardi called them "narrative structures" because "each consists of a network of lines and notations which are meant to convey a story, typically about a recent event of interest to me like the collapse of a large international bank, trading company or investment house. One of my goals," Lombardi continues, "is to map the interaction of political, social and economic forces in contemporary affairs."[108] He would meticulously research and gather information about real financial networks available in the public record, tracing relationships, interactions, and influences in graphite through lines, circles, and arrows. We find shady deals sketched, money laundered, taxes sheltered, arms traded and drugs trafficked, alliances formed between financial institutions, military bodies, politicians, business executives, terrorists, religious leaders, and gangsters. Lombardi would often expand and revise his network diagrams as new data became available to him, as one can see by following the serial versions of the "World Finance Corporation, Miami, ca. 1970–84" (made over the course of six years in the 1990s).

Lombardi developed a key explaining the graphic devices he used to make connections in his network representations: an arrow pointing in one direction indicating "some type of influence or control"; a two-way arrow indicating "some type of mutual relationship or association"; a dotted, directed arrow indicating "flow of money, loans, or credit"; jagged lines interrupting an arrow indicating "sale of transfer of an asset"; two vertical lines interrupting a dotted line indicating "blocked or incomplete transaction"; and a looping squiggled line indicating "the sale or spin-off of a property."[109] Some drawings layer information by using black and red to distinguish "essential elements of the story" from "major lawsuits, criminal indictments or other legal actions taken against the parties." As Anna Munster observes, "Lombardi's diagrams give us a sense not of the network per se but of *networking*— the processes and operations that join and separate disparate people and events along temporal horizons."[110] His network drawings are narratives only insofar as they unfold on the surface of the page *as* processes. They do not "abstract a set of ideal spatial relations between elements" but rather visualize "the contingent deformations and involutions of world events as they arise through conjunctive processes."[111] Many of Lombardi's networks cannot be isolated on any single page, but expand, shift time frames, and increase in detail from one version of the diagram to the next.

Robert Hobbs takes Lombardi to be intervening into (or "updat[ing]") the history of history painting, replacing "the tap-root theory" crucial to the genre—"that great individuals are the initiators of important events"—with one envisioning decentralized, rhizomatic, even chancy "channels of power."[112] If the narrative drawings are representations of history as such, their reductiveness, as much as their expansiveness, demands critical appraisal. There are no portraits, singular or group, in Lombardi's networks; there are names, dates, and abstract lines of influence. The sublimity of the history painting becomes purely mathematical. Their "network sublime," that is—an aesthetic response that emerges, Jagoda claims, from an experience of the magnitude of "big-data outputs" that can only be apprehended "partial[ly], tangential[ly], or asymptotic[ally]"—attacks our cognitive maps of global capital, drawing them out while offering a dizzying experience of complexity that severs our apprehension of events that follow linear cause and effect chain sequences.[113] Appropriately, scale, in much contemporary network art, becomes a thematic feature expressed in and by the form. Lars Bang Larsen, who has anthologized network art from the late twentieth century through the first decade-plus of the twenty-first, claims that networks and webs cease, once they become art as such, "to be instruments and infrastructure and can be acknowledged as phenomena that range across the infra, the macro and the in-between," joining the scales separating Lombardi's global financial flows and Pia Lindman's self-organizing fungal mold systems.[114]

Munster's "aesthesia of networks" finds contemporary diagrammatic and database art practices—from Lombardi's analog drawings to digital audiovisual *Gesamtkunstwerks*—producing novel, uncommon sensory fields. "Aesthetic novelty is borne on signs that are not yet known or sensed as such, on experience whose ground is only shifting durations and allopoietic loops."[115] Aestheticized networks "relationally prehend what is imperceptible." One virtue of Munster's aesthetics of network prehension is the somewhat surprising theoretical connection between our hyper-experience of networked life and the empirical psychology of William James. James's "radical empiricism" asserts "no bedding," no hard, unmovable ground to experience—"it is as if the pieces clung together by their edges, the transitions experienced between them forming their cement."[116] Edges and transitions; epistemic experience of the world cemented through relations and their joints. Munster's Jamesian keyword is "mosaic," a network form for experience that figures "the relations that allow thought to conjunctively expand."[117] For James, the mosaic is a cognitive form, naming the way thought- and perception-events transition between, attach to, and branch out from one another. "Experience itself, taken at large, can grow by its edges. That one moment of it proliferates into the next by transitions which, whether conjunctive or disjunctive, continue the experiential tissue, can not, I contend, be denied. Life is in the transitions as much as in the terms connected."[118] Going with "mosaic" instead of the more famous Jamesian stream of consciousness emphasizes a distributed pattern over a unidirectional flow.

So James's "radical empiricism," acutely understood, holds that relations between things—conjunctions, disjunctions, and the angles, complexities, strengths, and weaknesses of each—are as foundational to perceptual and cognitive experience as the things themselves, if not more so. "Mosaic" describes the movement of experienced relations, for James, rather than static wholes. The obvious analogy is to contemporary data visualization programs—the "mosaic plot" is a type of graph that visualizes relationships between at least two qualitative variables (unsurprisingly, Mosaic is also the name of a data science consultancy firm). Munster repurposes the concept of the "mosaic plot" in her look at Natalie Bookchin's 2009 video installation *Mass Ornament,* constructed from downloaded YouTube videos of people dancing in their homes, presented through overlapping, polyrhythmic arrays of video windows arranged as tiles on the screen. The just out of sync series of concatenated tiles creates the appearance of relay between dancers, their movements appearing to pass from one framed box to another—which also means from one part of the globe to another—without ever congealing into a neat conga line structure. Another example imposes itself through title alone: Stephen Soderbergh's 2017 murder mystery *Mosaic*.[119]

Initially released as an iOS/Android mobile app, *Mosaic* is an interactive episodic film where viewers (or viewer-users) actively personalize their narrative path by progressively selecting internal points of view on the murder mystery's fabula. The fabula does not itself change in response to viewer choices. You choose your own perspective on stable story events; that's the adventure. Which sounds like neither a film nor a novel, though Soderbergh claimed in an interview to be thinking of the latter, perhaps because even its traditional form offers more active control over the story's reception: *Mosaic*'s branching narrative network "will bring audiences a viewing experience similar to reading a novel."[120] And there is some novelistic paratext. Included alongside the story map which visualizes the narrative's nodal structure—including bifurcations and convergences—is a "Discoveries" option, where viewer-user-readers can find story-world documents like news reports, emails, and items from police files. But ultimately, *Mosaic* is only like a choose your own adventure novel—not a traditional realist (network) novel, even one with a paratextual map—where the adventure is in *who* you choose to follow and *how* doing so gives you an angle of knowledge about the stable story events.

And cinematically, *Mosaic* is more conventional than its project description suggests. Each scene is filmed multiple times to achieve several characters' points of view, which viewers encounter as different nodes on the story map. The Point-of-View (POV) shots are quite traditional; the difference from standard POV shots is that here, they are sutured into the fabula by one's understanding of the network structure rather than shot/reverse-shot, field/counter-field patterns. The differences one chooses as Soderbergh's partner-in-direction are not how to shoot the scripted written scene but whose point of view to emphasize—the technical result of the decision is really the way the scene's editing elides other possible perspectives, cutting out the reverse shots that would fill out a complete scene. It is a primitive form of interactive network cinema, perhaps, pushed into stylistic obsolescence only a year later by Charlie Brooker and David Slade's more nodally complex *Black Mirror: Bandersnatch* (2018), but preceded by an entire tradition of narrative gaming.

One of the biggest differences between participatory network narratives and what we might call their non-participatory counterparts is that time waits around for you in the former. This is evident even in single-player video games with nodal branches where players make narratively consequential decisions. Digital gaming involved navigating networks before multi-player video games extended their internal narrative forms to wider telecommunication networks. In his analysis of programs like Introversion's *Uplink* (2001), where gamers play as hackers taking on a series of contracts, Jagoda emphasizes the difference between the way digital games "model worlds and create microcosms of dynamic systems"—where players negotiate "the parameters of a designed system"—and the *represented* networks and microcosms of novels and feature films where interactivity is limited to cognitive reception.[121] While one can pause, rewind, and rewatch a film on video or DVD, and can control the pace of one's reading even more, the relations between syuzhet and fabula in traditional narrative forms are ultimately controlled by the text—readers and viewers actively process the spatial and durational terms set by the work. Even playing *The Legend of Zelda* on Nintendo 64, ten years old with a lot of time on my hands, I experienced something else entirely. I could stretch an afternoon exploring the game world's central hub, scavenging for items to trade or use in a future quest, knowing full well that the portals to the games within the game are all there waiting for me (*my* character) to pass through when I feel like it, to start the timers that clock the success or failure of the story's hero, which is also my avatar (though not a significantly personalized one). What happens exactly is not determined in advance, though the parameters and limits of narrative possibility are, in this case, set in stone.

The question of where gaming turns into simply living, or how much story control a game must have to qualify as a narrative viewed or read *rather than* life lived, is an important one we should not pass over too quickly in describing games as narratives. When something happens for the first time, do we call its event a narrative? Is a single pathway through a game world a narrative while it is being traversed, or only once it is recounted? Perhaps, definitionally, a lot depends on the relative presence or absence of a game master, which in traditional storytelling we might just call the author, real or implied. How much of the text is story, which involves representation, and how much is created moment-by-moment in the idiosyncratic acts of play? A narrative may be a "Garden of Forking Paths," but too much openness to the life of the reader or player and we are not talking about narrative at all anymore. I refer, of course, to Jorge Luis Borges's famous story, first published in 1941, which posits an unfinished book (*The Garden of Forking Paths*) written by a Chinese civil servant that reflects the author's "image of the universe":

> Unlike Newton and Schopenhauer, [Ts'ui Pen] did not believe in a uniform and absolute time; he believed in an infinite series of times, a growing, dizzying web of divergent, convergent and parallel times. That fabric of times that

approach one another, fork, are snipped off, or are simply
unknown for centuries, contains *all* possibilities. In most of
those times, we do not exist; in some, you exist but I do not;
in others, I do and you do not; in others still, we both do.[122]

Borges wrote the story more than a decade before physicist
Hugh Everett proposed his many-worlds interpretation of
quantum mechanics, positing a multiverse in which an infinite
number of divergent and non-communicating worlds exist in
quantum superposition. More important to the bibliophile
Borges's story than his character's ahead-of-its time many-
worlds theory of the universe is the way it is supposedly
replicated textually, in Ts'ui Pen's absolute mosaic fiction
(the complexity of which is compared favorably to the *Hung
Lu Meng*, a labyrinthine eighteenth-century Chinese classic
with over thirty main characters and several hundred minor
characters). In most fictions, "each time a man meets diverse
alternatives, he chooses one and eliminates all the others."[123]
But in Ts'ui Pen's novel, characters choose all of them, creating
several "futures" which in turn fork again, and again. Which
means the story is not just unfinished, but unfinishable (unlike,
we might note, Borges's short fiction of the same title). And
thus maybe it is not a story at all, but an exercise in the
conceptual limitation of story, or story perpetually discovering
its great outdoors.

Still, some writers have taken inspiration from Borges's
fable to try to replicate its promise in formats the brilliant
Argentine could have only dreamed (and probably did,
vaguely). Stuart Moulthrop, for example, whose electronic
novel *Victory Garden* (1992)—a clear reference to Borges, its
nodes cluster around the Gulf War rather than the First World
War—was one of several hypertext works produced around
the end of the century with the Storyspace software program.
Other notable titles include Michael Joyce's *afternoon, a story*
(1987), Deena Larsen's *Marble Springs* (1993), and Shelley
Jackson's *Patchwork Girl* (1995). Judy Malloy's *Its Name
Was Penelope* (original version from 1989) is another classic

of the genre, composed in Beginners' All-purpose Symbolic Instruction Code (BASIC). Robert Coover, delivering a keynote at what he perceived to be the sad end of literary hypertext's golden age in 1999, told of "pioneer narrative hypertexts" that "explored the tantalizing new possibility of laying a story out spatially instead of linearly, inviting the reader to explore it as one might explore one's memory or wander a many-pathed geographical terrain, and, being adventurous quests at the edge of a new literary frontier, they were often intensely self-reflective."[124] The hypertext novel's intense self-reflexivity is launched by the infrastructural complexity of the software. What Coover calls spatial composition is storytelling by digital cartography, which Storyspace affords by laying out the multiple paths by which a reader can reach a screen. In narratological terms: objective units of the story's fabula can exist in many possible places in the subjective order of the achieved syuzhet. The difference between the inside of the story world and its outside, moreover, is diminished to the point of dizzying complexity as other sites on the web are embedded as further possible pathways to explore through hyperlink. And as in video games, Storyspace allows writers to insert "guard fields" in the text, which deactivate links from one story unit or location to another until certain prerequisites or checkpoints are met. The simplest version of this is that one cannot proceed in one direction until one has read a specific sub-text or visited a certain story terrain, but the serial complexity of such preconditions may be dramatically amplified.

The most interesting hypertext authors are the ones who take best advantage of the software's non-linear mapping capacities. Or, as Coover puts it in a Miltonic phrase in an earlier *New York Times* article celebrating new digital narratives, those whose work offers "true freedom from the tyranny of the line," constructing kaleidoscopic mosaics where readers travel through a story to a provisional end without thereby exhausting (or even coming close to exhausting) the text's potentials for further diegesis.[125] There are always other paths through the text's topographical regions. *Victory Garden* is impossible to summarize, then. First because readers will move from a beginning to one possible end in a way very much their own, or at least statistically likely to be their own. Two native-language readers may differ completely in their interpretations of a sprawling Dickens or Tolstoy novel, though they should in principle agree on what the work literally contains. Not so in this case. Not even if two readers devoted all their free time to pursuing every plot permutation, since secondly, the text changes as one re-screens it.[126] To get the best sense one can of the whole plan, readers must move from the on-the-ground experience of navigating the story's links and its guard fields to the use of Storyspace's compass tool, which offers a map of adjacent nodes in cardinal directions and surface-depth relations between embedded levels in network clusters. But taking this supposed God's-eye view of the network takes one further away from the most intricate links governing the story world's main pathways (124 in *Victory Garden*), and the doors one may or may not pass through at times that are only definable by the specific narrative discourse constructed in and by the reading process.

Mosaics are ultimately defined by their part-whole relations, though the experiential procedure for passing from part to part and part to whole depends on the mode of its links. Traditional mosaics work at a spatial scale that anticipates the capacities and limitations of human eyes and the built space around the work. Whether you discern a whole pattern, an individual unit, or the latter bleeding into the former depends on how close you are to its surface and other embodied, environmental conditions, which interact with the materials used (tile, glass, stone, individual photographs, or whatever else). Digital mosaics—whether compositions, videos, stories, or games—may offer interactive options for proceeding from part to part and part to whole, like Soderbergh's tree or river delta form expressed in a paratextual map (a common feature of adventure games like *Zelda*). Somewhere between the traditional static mosaic and interactive ones are narratives that take a single, ultimate form. Feature films, novels, even operas. Giuseppe Verdi called some of his later works "mosaic dramas," like *The Force of Destiny* (*La forza del destino*), which episodically stitches a series of otherwise mismatched nineteenth-century operatic genres and styles together with the conceptual thread of his characters' destinies or fates (*destino*). The critical question is whether the units, put together in just this way, ever make a coherent pattern. And if not, why not? The difference between a designed network and a randomly generated one is that only one of them solicits the question about whether there is a good reason to form (or de-form) the network in the first place.

Chance, Contingency, Fate

"Things just happen." "*This* is something that happens." "There is no reason." It is not uncommon for a network film's most self-conscious character or first-person narrator to say stuff like this at quiet, introspective moments in the story. When it's time to take stock and reflect on the why: why something happens the way it does to people, which at the same time becomes an auto-reflexive "why networks?" The former is a question about life, its contingencies or determinacies (depending on one's worldview). The latter is a question about film, form, and narrative. The answers characters give need not be taken as moral taglines for the films they find themselves in, though sometimes advertising campaigns suggest as much (like *Crash*'s "Moving at the speed of life, we are bound to collide with each other"). The lines quoted above—taken from *Look Both Ways* (2005), *Magnolia* (1999), and *Thirteen Conversations About One Thing* (2001) respectively—are representative, but not quite self-explanatory. They are metaphysical theses about causality and existence that appeal to the texts their speakers are embedded in. But the texture of the film is just more thesis, never proof. Self-consciousness becomes a hall of mirrors, *mise en abyme*. Even if "things just happen" to people in the story world, without reason, at the level of the film's discourse or plotted form there are always reasons, or at least rhymes. The filmmakers made things this way, even put these lines in naïve characters' or semi-reliable narrators' mouths. So we are left with questions rather than answers: chance or fate? Is reality under- or overdetermined?

Chance, one might say, is the product of network complexity, and films that thematize chance and fate do so as if resulting from the narration's a priori decision to connect rather than isolate characters. What in life might "just happen" in a film must be carefully plotted. Take the reductio ad absurdum case, Greg Marck's *11:14* (2003). The digital clock readout title tells us which narrow slice of diegetic story time each plotline converges on, though the film's narrative structure takes us there five different ways. Our first encounter with the significance of that temporal nexus is the collision between a human body falling from an overpass and a passing driver's windshield. The character system that circulates around the initial plotted event is a small world, but the coincidences that lead us to the dramatic nexus of two different auto accidents multiply as more sections of the objective timeline, isolating new character groupings and locations in the town, are introduced. A Rube Goldberg machine made up of a severed penis, an accidental handgun discharge, an ill-planned robbery, an inauspicious graveyard decapitation, a poorly placed bowling ball, and an inopportune call on a cell phone gets us back to the beginning with, finally, a viable sense of the relevant interconnections that explain the initially inexplicable.

Coincidences, though, happen all the time. Only storytelling makes coincidences stand out from the ordinary baseline of any one thing after another. Aristotle defines chance in relation to the intended outcome of an event, like when pirates capture a sailor on his way to one city and take him to another.[127] Which means that chance occurrences or accidents happen relative to the causal stream of an intention. Whatever breaks in on the fulfillment of an intention has its own causal explanation; the pirates, after all, may be following their intentional scripts to the letter. If Aristotelian chance involves the impingement of one stream of action on another, we might say that narrative machines tuned to foreground the intersections of different causal-intentional streams are *formalizations* of chance. They highlight the contingency that grounds the ordinary. Network films sprawl outside the boundaries Aristotle set for well-unified plots—unities of space, time, and action—but may nevertheless depend on the fundamentals of plot as Aristotle articulates it in the *Poetics* (may even *especially* depend on them to achieve coherence amidst the sprawl): singular, seemingly contingent, and sometimes unexpected events, when seen together as parts of an unfolding whole, reveal causal or thematic links where there initially were few to none perceived.

Ask yourself how many coincidences and "chance" occurrences had to take place for you have done whatever specific thing you just did, whatever the time and wherever the place (the answer: an uncountable number). How many of those coincidences were, upon retrospection, narratively satisfying? Now that is an aesthetic question, one about the storyteller's art. Network narratives emphasize connections between characters or events at a distance. Connections between seemingly unrelated people or events are revealed non-linearly, mediated by relatively weak causal links. Or we might say, instead, that network narratives are *particularly good* at revealing the power of weak causal links, the fact that what often appears as action at a distance is in fact an invisible chain of micro-links that influences our immediate experience far more than we can ever adequately perceive. Every event in its unique singularity is the product of a near-zero probability of happening in just the way it does. Which means that the unlikely and the necessary collide every time the merely possible becomes actual: given Earth's population, one-in-a-million shots must pay off for almost 8,000 people. Chancy films like *11:14* squeeze into the gap opened up by a world where tightly woven causal networks produce unexpected collisions in short run temporal frames (in this case, marked by the minute), even though the law of large numbers and the human comedy of endlessness always tells us that the ordinary asserts itself over the long run. If every plot presents an infinitesimally small number of confluences in the wide story world in which its events take place, network narratives draw our attention to that fact, and reflect for us the narratological truth that every story succeeds or fails on the basis of selection and order and pattern rather than events themselves. On discourse, focalization, and narrational style. The surprising, unprecedented, or simply satisfying twist or turn is due to the pocket-sized slice of time and space covered by our experience. Narrative takes advantage of that fact, and network narratives take advantage of that advantage.

The awesomely bad 2004 speculative thriller *The Butterfly Effect* (dir. Eric Bress and J. Mackye Gruber) opens with an all-too-obvious epigraph, the famous Chinese proverb about a butterfly flapping its wings and thereby causing a massive and seemingly disproportionate event to erupt across the globe. The proverb is then propounded by the chaotic feedback loops played out in the film. Or is it? Unlike *11:14*, which reads like a marijuana-fueled, adolescent Mouse Trap boardgame set up for the fun of it, *The Butterfly Effect* is one of those network films that protests too much. Though it has a clear protagonist, played by Ashton Kutcher, the film's time travel feature thematizes the densely woven causal chains linking its small world of characters together. Every time he goes back in time to undo the tragic result of an event in the group's traumatic past, the change in the master narrative produces an unexpected consequence, always somehow even worse than the original timeline, as if to suggest life was originally as good as it could ever get.

A procession of non-linear feedback loops leads to narrative chaos. (For a compelling if far less popular counterexample, *Bug* [2002, dir. Phil Hay and Matt Manfredi], which shares in narrative philosophy of small causes and disproportionately scaled effects, offers a tight causal chain of cascading events originating in the simple act of a child stepping on an insect. This conceit allows the film to network a larger number of characters in a coherent and convergent way, while *The Butterfly Effect*'s temporal loops endlessly revise the fates of a much smaller cohort.) We must assume that either this is the unluckiest group of people who have ever lived, or there is some guiding moral consciousness floating above the action, unmotivated by the film's plot logic: thou shalt not wish things turned out better. Ultimately, Kutcher's Evan travels back one last time to fix their fates by cutting off the initial social network entirely. Depending on which ending you have—the theatrical and director's cuts differ, and you can choose either with the DVD—he either insults his friend Kayleigh early enough in their lives so that they will never speak to each other again, or he goes back even further in objective time and strangles himself with his own umbilical cord in the womb, so that he's never even born. The ultimate choice, then, is between endlessly reshuffling the doomed network or making it never have existed in the first place.

One of the many problems with *The Butterfly Effect* is that its network form contains a loophole that negates its thematic motivation: not only is there a protagonist, but he is so narratively self-conscious that he transcends the network that the film asks us to believe is untranscendable. He has the gift of remembering and being able to compare timelines, though nobody else in the story world can. In that sense Evan is like us, watching the film and aware of all the causal chains and alternative pathways explored, while everyone else is like us when we are just living our lives. He is only partially enmeshed in a world otherwise governed by thick entanglement—the narrative procedure would not "work" otherwise. In reality, there are a lot of butterflies flapping their wings every second. Despite itself, then, *The Butterfly Effect* divulges a paradox of network form in general. Expressed as a single identifiable nexus of narrative multiplicity, network films straddle the divide between idiosyncratic storytelling modes and conventional cinematic discourse. They must, if they want a dizzying array of tangential lives and events to track for viewers whose folk bases for storying are grounded in linear causality. *The Butterfly Effect* depends on cliches about doomed-to-this-world teenage love and stock-in-trade childhood traumas straight out of the wholesale box; it depends on time-tested sci-fi time travel conventions about the relationships between past, present, and future; it depends on a three-act structure with a double-length middle to keep the proliferation of alternative micro-plots from spinning out of episodic control. All narratives filter out chaos even when contingency is a theme. More coherent forking paths narratives like *Run Lola Run*, *Sliding Doors*, and *Blind Chance* find ways to reduce possible story thresholds to a small cluster of nodes, ultimately revealing the impossibility of telling a story of truly chaotic multiplicity.

But true chance only exists in narrative when life itself is inserted into the equation as a variable, even when circumscribed by pathways—like in games, or in choose your own adventures. Network and forking path plot structures suggest what they cannot really deliver, and in doing so mark the limits of narrative as such. Even when chance seems to dictate characters' fates, narration still dictates, and fate rules by the fiat of filmmakers' choice. Every network film, then, is a conspiracy film, but as form rather than content, since there is a guiding hand controlling every accident, a deeper intelligence behind the screened surface. That is what separates network narratives from networked life, where conspiracies are often psychological rather than structural truths.[128] And yet network films craft the contradiction between control and freedom amidst inevitable interconnection into plot, showing how free action is overdetermined by forces and protocols unviewable within single experiential frames, but at least partially mappable once those frames come into contact. And perhaps only fully knowable from the standpoint of an algorithm or a massive data set; in other words, by databases rather than narratives.

Accidents, convergences, and unforeseen collisions may seem to interrupt and ultimately disrupt conventional goal-obstacle-deadline-free choice plot pathways, but network forms assert their own conventions too, from small-world ensembles revealed tangentially to the thematic attention given to chance and coincidence as a cosmic, metaphysical, or simply social condition. Narrational selection, ordering, and emphasis stand behind events of chance in any story, and every story contains events uncontrolled or unmanifested by its characters' wills. The more chaotic the plot strands are, the more narratorial emphasis on time, place, privileged causal junctures, or bridge motifs is needed to make the whole cohere. *11:14* is not just the name of a film, but a diegetic signpost, a revealed reading on clocks in every timeline, offered to the viewer through short but necessary windows of cinematic omniscience. *11:14* is a chance nexus of colliding fates, but it is also a principle of network narration. It is not just the vortex toward which all the action tends in the world of the story, but—and despite the dramatic difference between the order in the story world and the chaotic shifts between temporal points and character foci in the discourse—the necessary signifier that repeatedly sutures the facts of that world together. It gives us a chance to comprehend.

Omniscience?

Every narrative structure generates corresponding narrational pressures, apertures onto the action and diegetic world appropriately tuned to the story form. Henry James's great metaphor for his "house of fiction," which has "not one window, but a million," at each of which stands "a figure with a pair of eyes, or at least with a field-glass," articulates the novelist's sense of narrative as a spatial edifice outfitted with a series of bounded points of view on the world it contains.[129] James offered cinema a great metaphor *avant la lettre*. Film, of course, is more literally a medium for seeing than literary fiction. One could imagine Metro-Goldwyn-Mayer(MGM)'s *Grand Hotel* conceived as a building with many windows, looking *in* at the characters' slices of reality, where the implied viewer is serially posted. The windows may be in motion (the metaphor has its limitations), but the art of the shot is in the first instance an art of organizing and framing partial views.

There is nothing about network cinema that guarantees the types of shots or depths of field that offer us access to its diegesis. Its apertures may crop its individual characters and their pathways closely or its scenes may rely on long, wide, moving master shots where important details are slowly searched for and discovered (a tendency Altman was well known to employ). But there is a tendency toward narratorial omniscience in network film. Not in every way, to be sure; network films often make us feel that we know its characters and their motivations more obliquely than we do traditional protagonists'. But cinema—unlike the novel, with its capacities for quoted monologues, narrated monologues, and free indirect discourse—rarely gets us "inside" any character's head in the first place, POV shots and voice-overs notwithstanding. Network form, I believe, is the closest narrative film comes to free indirect discourse, which in literary prose blends the narrator's voice with the fiction's characters, so that it is impossible to say where one ends and the other begins. Since network films need not (and most often do not) narrate through spoken or written language, this is only an analogy. But hopefully a useful one.

At first, each character-node in a network film seems to be selected by the film's narration more arbitrarily than traditional protagonists are, since the conceit of a protagonist-driven film is that *this* person or *this* couple, though one among many in the story world, is especially worthy of our attention. We often know everything we need to know about them early on—their desires, their flaws, their backstories—though the film's syuzhet may conceal a few bits of information until late in the movie, as in the case of a flashback or a revealed secret that makes retroactive sense of an event or a complex motivation. But the price of that knowledge is paid by a corresponding lack of narratorial omniscience of the wider story world, of things going on and other potential characters—things presumably happening and people presumably living, if we are to assume a coherently realistic universe—only tangentially linked to the protagonists and their plot path.

Bordwell thinks that network narration "tends toward omniscience" because of its "shared-time principle."[130] Whether the network departs from, converges upon, or never delivers a plot nexus, there is no guarantee that characters in a network film will fall in love, become friends, become enemies, or even meet one another at all. Network narration works best when it hides the seams of its stitches to bring multiple inner perspectives on the story world into meaningful, seemingly inevitable contact (if not always synthesis). Omniscience may be measured by how long and fine the gossamer fibrils connecting one person to another are—so long as they don't break. But there is still always a possibility, in network narratives, of withheld or delayed information, just like in any other narrative discourse. So it might make more sense to say that network narration makes the *problem* of omniscience explicit. When we know that everything and everyone is connected, but we do not immediately know how or why, we start to speculate. We ask the questions fundamental to any and every act of human storytelling: Why these people, and why there and then, and why do they interact with each other in this particular way?

Bordwell also claims that "sideways-shifting tales," narratives that pull us side to side in a network rather than incessantly forward toward a climax or resolution, "push us to reflect on how filmic storytelling works."[131] I do not think network films are necessarily *primary* in this regard, and I do not think Bordwell thinks so either (his interest in noirs and detective stories as meta-narratological texts suggests as much). But we might theorize that since all films that imply a coherent story world depend on us, the viewer, to infer and reconstruct that world with the information given, networks are at least one of the cinematic forms well suited to reflect on how narrational omniscience is made. Form and content reinforce each other here, given how many network films make modern, urban life thematic. In the modern city, in modern transport, and even in cyberspace we bump into, collide with, come into conflict with, or simply brush by more people, more places, and more landmarks than ever before. Still, as individuals, we only ever occupy one moving vantage of that crowded world. It is no wonder Wendy Everett, in an essay on "fractal films" (each example of which we might also call a network film), arrives at the feet of Michel de Certeau and his "practice of everyday life," particularly his study of spatial practices like walking through the twentieth-century city.[132]

We might say that the syntax of network films—the way their parts hang together—follows from the infrastructure of modern, urban, industrial life. The network of characters and interwoven plots overlays infrastructural networks that lubricate the movements and flows of everyday life. But network form reveals those infrastructures (both public and private) which we normally take for granted, that do the socially unconscious work of connection: roadways and sidewalks and public transportation, public utilities, the circulation of goods in the marketplace, common places and spaces, apartment complexes, and hotels and hangouts. Social infrastructures tend to do more explicit work in narratives that connect characters and events through sideways steps in the discourse rather than at waystations along a protagonist's main line of action and development. As I will discuss in the next chapter, the traffic accident is such a useful convention in network films because it is a readymade scenario for chance convergences, built into the background of modern life in a way that lessens the need for additional narratorial motivation. Other infrastructural networks can do the job too, though: public housing (Eric Khoo's *12 Storeys*, 1997); trains (Jean-Claude Guiguet's *The Passengers*, 1999); supply chains (Richard Linklater's *Fast Food Nation*, 2006); a school campus (Matsuo Yanigimachi's *Who's Camus Anyway?*, 2006); a radio station (Anthony Wong's *Top Banana Club*, 1996); public event space (Johannes Brunner's *Oktoberfest*, 2005); medical facilities (Lee Sholem's *Emergency Hospital*, 1956); and so on.

Narratives generate omniscience effects whenever their discourses disclose more diegetic information than is reasonably available within any single character's focal field. For omniscience to be a useful term for film theory, we must see it as a scale rather than an all-or-nothing category, which admittedly challenges the word's literal meaning (Can one be somewhat all knowing? Omniscient within prescribed limits?). Extreme long shots generate a certain amount of narratorial omniscience, but crosscutting generates even more, and large-scale plot structures that shift focus between characters effect even more still. I call those large-scale formal devices infrastructures because they ground character networks and make them work. They supply narratorial logics that widen our attentional field beyond the protagonist's narrow path without sacrificing story coherence altogether. Network narratives trade some of the coherence banked by protagonist-driven forms, in other words, for alternative magnetizers: shared spaces or locations; shared timespans; events or occasions for gathering; circulating objects; families or friend groups or coworker pods; types of people, occupations, affects, or life experiences that join characters and storylines conceptually as examples or specimens. They must find at least one unifying principle to manage the larger formal distribution, as if paying ahead of time for the spread of the network with the promise of a hard border around the represented world, limits within which the expansiveness of its discourse must remain. Like having complete freedom to go wild, as long as you stay in the sandbox with your three toys.

We will have the chance to extend our thinking on network form in the next chapter, digging deeper into one text instead of skating swiftly over a still-expanding field of theoretical knowledge. In gradually shifting my attention from a few intellectual nodes of a general network theory to some of the formal and narratological basics of network narratives in this chapter, I have tried to establish the grounds upon which we can establish a fuller reading of an exceptional (though by no means totally representative) network film. As I tighten focus on Altman's *Nashville*, my analysis will become more cinematic, bringing cinematography, sound, editing, and other specifically filmic features into the conversation. Just as theory can serve film, film can serve theory. *Nashville* does its own network thinking, in ways unique to the capacities of audiovisual media. I am not an omniscient narrator, not even close. And *Nashville* is not about everything network theorists care about, not even close. Relations go on forever, but our diagrams and maps must stop somewhere. There are worse places to end up than at the Grand Ole Opry.

Notes

1 Frigyes Karinthy, "Chain-Links," trans. Adam Makkai, in *The Structure and Dynamics of Networks,* ed. Mark Newman, Albert-László Barabási, and Duncan J. Watts (Princeton: Princeton University Press, 2006), 22.
2 Ibid., 21.
3 Ibid., 22.
4 Ibid., 23.
5 Ibid., 24.
6 Ibid.
7 David Bordwell, *Poetics of Cinema* (New York: Routledge, 2008), 190–1.
8 Evan Smith, "Thread Structure: Rewriting the Hollywood Formula," *Journal of Film and Video* 51.3–4 (Fall/Winter 1999/2000): 88.
9 Ibid.
10 Kristin Thompson, *Storytelling in the New Hollywood: Understanding Classical Narrative Technique* (Cambridge, MA: Harvard University Press, 1999), 12.
11 Ibid., 14.
12 Ibid., 74.
13 See María del Mar Azcona, *The Multi-Protagonist Film* (Oxford: Wiley-Blackwell, 2010), 37–8.
14 Émile Durkheim, *The Rules of Sociological Method,* trans. W. D. Halls, in *The Rules of Sociological Method and Selected*

Texts on Sociology and Its Method, ed. Steven Lukes (London: Macmillan, 1982), 50.
15 Ibid., 56.
16 Ibid., 59.
17 Adam Smith, *The Theory of Moral* Sentiments, ed. Knud Haakonssen (Cambridge: Cambridge University Press, 2009), 11.
18 The Victorian Herbert Spencer was a forerunner, whether Durkheim acknowledged the extent or not, in articulating sociological principles on the basis of grasping "the vast heterogeneous aggregate, as to see how each [social] group is at each stage determined partly by its own antecedents and partly by the past and present actions of the rest upon it" (Spencer, *The Principles of Sociology,* Vol. I [London: Williams & Norgate, 1876], 462). Mary Poovey has tracked the longer, slower migration of the English word "social," initially used exclusively as an adjective applied to individuals, toward its wide use in nominal forms. These etymological shifts point to "the rise of modern abstraction, that complex series of theoretical and institutional developments by which particular abstractions (like 'society' and 'the economy') acquired sufficient institutional presence to become trans-individual entities with real material effects" (Poovey, "The Liberal Civil Subject and the Social in Eighteenth-Century British Moral Philosophy," in *The Social in Question*, ed. Patrick Joyce [London: Routledge, 2001], 47).
19 Durkheim, 40 (emphasis in original).
20 Ibid., 39.
21 Conversely, sociological emphasis on crime to the point of statistical obsession perhaps reveals the ultimate concern and anxiety about the efficacy of social structures. If suicide is the existential choice *par excellence*, crime is the social fact that most compellingly tests the limits of social authority. And if crime can be shown to be internal to sociocultural life (rather than simply outside of it, or in complete rejection of its compacts), sociology can authorize its own authority as a universal human discipline with extraordinary explanatory power.
22 Alexander R. Galloway and Eugene Thacker, *The Exploit: A Theory of Networks* (Minneapolis: University of Minnesota Press, 2013), 26.

23 Caroline Levine, *Forms: Whole, Rhythm, Hierarchy, Network* (Princeton: Princeton University Press, 2017), 117.
24 Ibid., 118.
25 Franco Moretti, *Atlas of the European Novel: 1800–1900* (London: Verso, 1999).
26 Ibid., 113.
27 Ibid., 124–9.
28 Ibid., 130.
29 Charles Dickens, *Bleak House: An Authoritative and Annotated Text,* ed. George Ford and Sylvere Monod (New York: W. W. Norton, 1977), 197.
30 Patrick Jagoda, *Network Aesthetics* (Chicago: University of Chicago Press, 2016), 3.
31 Ibid., 13.
32 Manuel Castells, *The Rise of the Network Society*, 2nd ed. (Chichester: Wiley-Blackwell, 2010), 77.
33 Castells, *The Internet Galaxy: Reflections on the Internet, Business, and Society* (New York: Oxford University Press, 2001), 87.
34 Galloway, *Protocol: How Control Exists after Decentralization* (Cambridge, MA: MIT Press, 2006), 3.
35 Gilles Deleuze, "Postscript on Control Societies," in *Negotiations: 1972–1990*, trans. Martin Joughin (New York: Columbia University Press, 1995), 177.
36 Ibid., 178–9.
37 Ibid., 179–80.
38 Wendy Hui Kyong Chun, *Control and Freedom: Power and Paranoia in the Age of Fiber Optics* (Cambridge, MA: MIT Press, 2008), 9.
39 Norbert Wiener, *Cybernetics: Or, Control and Communication in the Animal and Machine* (New York: Wiley, 1948).
40 Tiziana Terranova, *Network Culture: Politics for the Information Age* (London: Pluto Press, 2004), 55–6.
41 Ibid., 56.
42 Steven Shaviro, *Connected, or What It Means to Live in the Network Society* (Minneapolis: University of Minnesota Press, 2003), ix.
43 Ibid., 109.
44 Adam Greenfield, *Everyware: The Dawning Age of Ubiquitous Computing* (Berkeley: New Riders, 2010), 1, 16.

45 David Harvey, *The Condition of Postmodernity: An Enquiry into the Origins of Cultural Change* (London: Blackwell, 1989), 156.
46 Henry James, *The Art of the Novel: Critical Prefaces*, ed. Richard P. Blackmur (New York: Scribner, 1978), 5.
47 Virginia Woolf, *The Essays of Virginia Woolf*, ed. Andrew McNellie, 6 vols. (San Diego: Harcourt, 1986–2011), 2:348.
48 T. S. Eliot, "On Henry James," in *The Question of Henry James*, ed. F. W. Dupee (New York: Henry Holt, 1945), 110.
49 See Georg Lukács, *The Theory of the Novel: A Historico-philosophical Essay on the Forms of Great Epic Literature*, trans. Anna Bostock (Cambridge, MA: MIT Press, 1971).
50 Duncan J. Watts, *Six Degrees: The Science of a Connected Age* (New York: Norton, 2004), 83.
51 Jagoda, 75.
52 Fredric Jameson, *Postmodernism, or, The Cultural Logic of Late Capitalism* (Durham: Duke University Press, 1991), 51.
53 Louis Althusser, "Ideology and Ideological State Apparatuses," in *Lenin and Philosophy and Other* Essays, trans. Ben Brewster (New York: Monthly Review Press, 1971), 162.
54 Vivien Silvey, "Not Just Ensemble Films: Six Degrees, Webs, Multiplexity and the Rise of Network Narratives," *Forum* 8 (Spring 2009), https://doi.org/10.2218/forum.08.621.
55 Jagoda, 76.
56 Stephen Farber, "A Half-Dozen Ways to Watch the Same Movie," *New York Times* (November 13, 2005), https://www.nytimes.com/2005/11/13/movies/a-halfdozen-ways-to-watch-the-same-movie.html.
57 Charles Ramírez Berg, "A Taxonomy of Alternative Plots in Recent Films: Classifying the 'Tarantino Effect,'" *Film Criticism* 31.1/2 (2006): 18.
58 Perhaps the biggest problem was, as Judith Kleinfeld observes, an obvious methodological bias that skewed results toward smaller chains. Longer paths were underrepresented in the results because they were more likely to break off along the chain, never reach their destination, and thus not be counted in the average (see Kleinfeld, "Six Degrees: Urban Myth?," *Psychology Today* [March 2002]). Then again, in the opposite direction, we also cannot be sure that participants did in fact select acquaintances accurately (i.e., the ones actually closest,

in the shortest chain, to the target individual). We do not necessarily know who knows whom, and so might have shorter paths through our social networks than we realize. Which is a problem, since the experiment aimed to measure shortest average degrees of social relation regardless of any one person's ability to reconstruct them in toto.
59 See Mark Buchanan, *Nexus: Small Worlds and the Groundbreaking Science of Networks* (New York: Norton, 2002), 114.
60 Galloway and Thacker, 33–4.
61 Ibid., 33.
62 Ibid., 34.
63 Ibid.
64 Sergey Brin and Lawrence Page, "The Anatomy of a Large-Scale Hypertextual Web Search Engine," *Computer Networks and ISDN Systems* 30 (1998): 111.
65 Ibid., 107.
66 John Durham Peters, *The Marvelous Clouds: Toward a Philosophy of Elemental Media* (Chicago: University of Chicago Press, 2015), 327.
67 Albert-László Barabási, *Linked: The New Science of Networks* (Cambridge: Perseus, 2002), 71.
68 Ibid., 167.
69 Ibid., 168–9.
70 Ibid., 77.
71 Franco Moretti, "Network Theory, Plot Analysis," *Stanford Literary Lab* Pamphlet 2 (May 1, 2011): 3.
72 James Stiller, Daniel Nettle, and Robin I. M. Dunbar, "The Small World of Shakespeare's Plays," *Human Nature* 14.4 (2003): 399 (emphasis added).
73 Moretti, 3.
74 Ibid., 11.
75 Ibid., 3–4.
76 See Alex Woloch, *The One vs. the Many: Minor Characters and the Space of the Protagonist in the Novel* (Princeton: Princeton University Press, 2003).
77 Bruno Latour, *The Pasteurization of France,* trans. Alan Sheridan and John Law (Cambridge, MA: Harvard University Press, 1993), 162.
78 Ibid., 163.

79 Graham Harman, *Prince of Networks: Bruno Latour and Metaphysics* (Melbourne: re.press, 2009), 13.
80 Bruno Latour, *Reassembling the Social: An Introduction to Actor-Network-Theory* (Oxford: Oxford University Press, 2005), 12.
81 Ibid., 4–5.
82 Ibid., 1.
83 Ibid., 1, 3.
84 Christopher Herbert, *Culture and Anomie: Ethnographic Imagination in the Nineteenth Century* (Chicago: University of Chicago Press, 1991), 4–5.
85 William Mazzarella, *The Mana of Mass Society* (Chicago: University of Chicago Press, 2017), 1.
86 Ibid., 4.
87 Latour, *Reassembling the Social*, 124.
88 Ibid., 131.
89 Bruno Latour, *We Have Never Been Modern,* trans. Catherine Porter (Cambridge, MA: Harvard University Press, 1993), 10, my emphasis.
90 Harman, 14.
91 Bruno Latour, "On Technical Mediation," *Common Knowledge* 3.2 (1994): 32.
92 Harman, 18.
93 Latour, *Reassembling the Social*, 44.
94 Ibid., 217.
95 Latour, *We Have Never Been Modern*, 112.
96 Ibid., 3.
97 Latour, *Reassembling the Social*, 65.
98 Ibid., 53.
99 David J. Krieger and Andréa Belliger, *Interpreting Networks: Hermeneutics, Actor-Network Theory & New Media* (New York: Columbia University Press, 2014), 107.
100 Alf Hornborg, "Artifacts have Consequences, Not Agency: Toward a Critical Theory of Global Environmental History," *European Journal of Social Theory* 20.1 (2017): 4.
101 Bill Brown, *A Sense of Things: The Object Matter of American Literature* (Chicago: University of Chicago Press, 2003), 4.
102 Karl Marx, "Capital, Volume One," in *The Marx-Engels Reader,* 2nd ed., ed. Robert C. Tucker (New York: W. W. Norton, 1978), 319.
103 Brown, 39.

104 Harman, 104.
105 Ibid., 116.
106 Latour, *Reassembling the Social,* 142.
107 See Sianne Ngai on this point in Latour in "Network Aesthetics," in *American Literature's Aesthetic Dimensions*, ed. Cindy Weinstein and Christopher Looby (New York: Columbia University Press, 2012), 367–92.
108 Mark Lombardi, "The Recent Drawings: An Overview," *Cabinet Magazine* 2 (Spring 2001): n.p.
109 Robert Carleton Hobbs and Mark Lombardi, *Global Networks* (New York: Independent Curators International, 2004), 52.
110 Anna Munster, *An Aesthesia of Networks: Conjunctive Experience in Art and Technology* (Cambridge, MA: MIT Press, 2013), 4.
111 Ibid., 4–5.
112 Robert Hobbs, "Mark Lombardi: Global Networks," in *Networks*, ed. Lars Bang Larsen (Cambridge, MA: MIT Press, 2014), 200.
113 Jagoda, 48–9.
114 Lars Bang Larsen, "Introduction: The Unimaginable Globality of Networks," in *Networks,* ed. Lars Bang Larsen (Cambridge, MA: MIT Press, 2014), 12.
115 Munster, 10.
116 William James, *Essays in Radical Empiricism* (New York: Longmans Green, 1912), 86.
117 Munster, 32.
118 James, *Radical Empiricism*, 87.
119 I am grateful to Gitanjali Kapila for raising this example and discussing it at length with me. She precedes me in her analysis of *Mosaic*.
120 Paraphrased from Soderbergh's live interview with Elvis Mitchell by Chris O'Falt, "'Mosaic': Steven Soderbergh Unveils the Three-Year Process of Making His 7-Hour HBO Experiment," IndieWire (October 6, 2017), https://www.indiewire.com/features/general/mosiac-steven-soderbergh-hbo-interactive-branching-narrative-1201884623/.
121 Jagoda, 148.
122 Jorge Luis Borges, "The Garden of Forking Paths," in *Collected Fictions,* trans. Andrew Hurley (New York: Penguin Books, 1998), 127.
123 Ibid., 125.

124 Robert Coover, "Literary Hypertext: The Passing of the Golden Age," *FEED* (February 10, 2000), http://www.feedmag.com/document/do291.shtml.
125 Robert Coover, "The End of Books," *The New York Times* (June 21, 1992), https://archive.nytimes.com/www.nytimes.com/books/98/09/27/specials/coover-end.html.
126 See Robert L. Selig's account of his repeated readings of Moulthrop's novel for a sense of this experience ("The Endless Reading of Fiction: Stuart Moulthrop's Hypertext Novel *Victory Garden*," *Contemporary Literature* 41.4 [Winter 2000]: 642–60). He reports that it took him a hundred or so screenings before he felt the diminishing returns in the narrative shifts and stopped re-reading it, though he did not come close to exhausting its pathway combinations.
127 Aristotle, "Metaphysics," in *The Complete Works of Aristotle: The Revised Oxford Translation*, Vol. 2, ed. Jonathan Barnes (Princeton: Princeton University Press, 1984), V.1025.26–30, 1619.
128 On this point I differ from Jagoda in his reading of *Syriana*. See Jagoda, 100.
129 Henry James, *The Portrait of a Lady: An Authoritative Text*, ed. Robert D. Bamberg (New York: W. W. Norton, 1975), 7.
130 Bordwell, 200.
131 Ibid., 191.
132 Wendy Everett, "Fractal Films and the Architecture of Complexity," *Studies in European Cinema* 2.3 (2005): 168.

CHAPTER 2

What Is *Nashville*?

Everything Runs in Circles

You must enter a network *in medias res*. There are no lighted entrances and exits, no marked rest stops along its thruways. But that might not be quite true of a film, no matter how networked in form and structure. There is, after all, a beginning and an end to its runtime. Even when chance plays a larger than typical role in its path to the final cut. And there is, one might say, a linear flow of frames and scenes from one end to the other, even when linearity has been strained just shy of its breaking point. These are true statements, at least, about the film whose network we enter now: Robert Altman's *Nashville*.

Altman did not walk into the *Nashville* project at its beginning. Or not exactly. In 1972 United Artists handed him a script for a film to be titled *The Great Southern Amusement Company*. It was to center around the *Nashville* music scene and was to be a vehicle for the pop baritone Tom Jones. Altman did not like country music and did not see much merit in the script. The writing stunk. He said he would make a film, a different film about Nashville, if the studio would finance the movie he wanted to make first, *Thieves Like Us*. A deal was struck, and Altman tabbed collaborator Joan Tewkesbury to write a new script. While Altman was shooting *Thieves* in Mississippi, Tewkesbury scouted the city of Nashville, wandering about from recording studio to performance venue in search of a form that would organize a film about a city and its culture.

Before trying to understand how significant Tewkesbury's method and Altman's complementary directorial tendencies would be for something we have since come to call network film, I should say something about Hollywood scripts first. In the early days of silent cinema, scripts as we know them now did not exist. Constance Collier, at one time an extra in D. W. Griffith's *Intolerance* (1916), later said that Griffith "never had a scenario, but would take miles and miles of film that never saw the light of day," all the while holding "in his brain the continuity of the story."[1] When major studios like Metro-Goldwyn-Mayer Studios Inc. (M. G. M.) consolidated the factory conditions that governed filmmaking in Hollywood's Golden Age, one of its instruments was the stability of the script. Which is not to say scripts never changed; they certainly did. But the rise of what David Thomson calls the script "as a sacred thing" coincided with and assisted the rise of the hierarchical studio system.[2] It was a way of taking the film's vision out of the mind of the mad genius, away from the Griffiths and the Stroheims whose personal aesthetic obsessions threatened budgets and the studio's political and aesthetic commitments, which increasingly became financial models. The script as an institutional principle kept would-be auteurs and their irresponsible desires in line.

As the screenplay rose in power, so came the occasional desire to subvert its formats. That's one way to interpret what Altman and Tewkesbury were up to in the early days of writing *Nashville* into existence. The coin's flip side is Tewkesbury's admitted lack of knowledge about country music, and Altman's desire to throw a talented writer with a nomadic track record of mainstream pursuits into an unknown sociocultural world with a complicated history, to have her walk around in it, progressively filling in a blank cognitive map. On her second attempt at visiting Music City for material, Tewkesbury immediately ran into a crush at Nashville airport.[3] A crowd of fans waited impatiently on the tarmac for a star musician to arrive on a private plane. News teams swarmed. And awaiting her on the freeway, the channel of hopes for all manner of American freedom and futurity and exit velocity, was a gnarly pileup.

The dense network of Nashville music culture, with its edges touching some larger web of Americana, appeared at first like a knot for Tewkesbury to patiently (and frustratingly) disentangle. Acerbically, she expressed a parallel sense of part-to-whole fabric in the film she was sent to help make and the social network the same film would try to map: "the whole piece was about people who were trying to do the best job they could with the equipment they had in this dumb kind of social structure."[4] We can take her reference to "equipment" literally. Tewkesbury's Nashville trip was organized around the cultural hubs of music production and distribution: studios, recording sessions, live performances. She saw Loretta Lynn and Conway Twitty record; she saw the Fisk Jubilee Singers. She interviewed technicians and engineers, witnessed radio broadcasts in progress, and visited a country memorabilia museum with Patsy Cline's hairpins on display. And at the venue Exit/In, she reported a spatio-geometric revelation:

> There were several people I had seen throughout the day. The city is built in a circle, so if I saw you in the morning and didn't know who you were, I'd see you at least two times before the end of the day. I walked outside after a couple of hours in this joint and I looked up and there was a full moon. I said, "Shit, everything runs in circles in this town." I said, "Fuck, this is it. It's all about overlaps and connective tissue."[5]

The shape of the city shapes Tewkesbury's narrative schema. Like a wandering Ralph Waldo Emerson transported to the 1970s South, she saw Nashville as circles within circles, some interacting like moving Venn diagrams, some connected at a distance through sound waves in the air, all of them mediated by recording equipment.

Because understanding how a network works (how its net *works*) means figuring how it was formed and continues to re-form itself across the span of its existence, this chapter unfolds somewhat like a Tewksburian walking tour of *Nashville* (the film, not the city). With the caveat that the Nashville of *Nashville*—the cultural locus, the late twentieth-century American mind-space—is a moving, dynamic complexity. As in the evolution of the film's script, which ended up serving as a starting point for heavily improvised scenes, all cognitive maps we form of the movie's diegetic lifeworld unfold like shifting panoramas. They broach, if not breach, the subliminal energies connecting ostensibly distant characters and events, asking us to let much that goes unseen enter our roving picture frames. Which, in fact, is a not-half-bad definition of cinematic interpretation.

"Count 'Em"

"Let me go directly to the point." So begins a running campaign speech, and the film it hopes to entwine with the dreams of Hal Phillip Walker's vision for America. Neither will go directly to or even toward a point. "I'm for doing some replacing." So says the voice from the Replacement Party van's Public Address system. Opening on Walker's campaign van leaving the garage of his Tennessee State Headquarters, we wonder what needs replacing, or what in the world of *Nashville* will be replaced (and by what or whom). It is an obscure wish, one for all of America to consider.

But wait. I jumped ahead a bit. The film really opens on an advertisement for itself. In the opening credit sequence a record jacket spins out of a black screen void, beginning an imitation of a K-tel record infomercial. You can probably hear the compilation album salesman's voice and its hard-sell cadence now: "Now(!), after years in the making, Robert Altman brings the big screen the long-awaited *Nashville*, with twenty-four—count 'em—twenty-four of your very favorite stars!" A lot starts happening at once. The adman rolls through the twenty-four names—the stars, *Nashville*'s cast—as close-ups of their cartoon caricatures from the jacket cycle through the center of the frame, behind which circle individual photographic album covers featuring the same cast. On the left side of the frame cast credits scroll up, while on the right side the song titles that make up the film's soundtrack (performed in the film to come by the characters played by this cast) scroll down in smaller font. And brief samples from the songs play all the while, layered alongside the announcer's voice in the mix. Periodically the film's title flashes diagonally atop the collage.

Only the opening credits, one might say—really the pre-credits—but it is an exceptionally self-reflexive set piece. For one, the spot suggests that the film to follow is a means for selling the soundtrack, the kind of merchandising program soon to take over Hollywood production logic with George Lucas's *Star Wars* deal. The chaotic over-and-under-layering, all assembled on the shallow plane of infomercial space,

FIGURE 2 *"Now, after years in the making . . ." All film stills are taken from* Nashville *directed by Robert Altman © Paramount Pictures 1975. All rights reserved.*

offers a kaleidoscopic key to *Nashville*'s ontological structure. Artifice is braided tightly through the warp of the real, like the cartoon caricatures superimposed atop their photographic likenesses, and the actors-performers' names balancing (albeit asymmetrically, like a seesaw with more weight on one side) the song titles they perform as characters.[6] The film's character network is presented as both totality and mass confusion. It is an intelligible, numbered system and a flickering jumble, a panorama and a fractured heap. Each character is equally person and persona. And the world they all live in, we gather, is commodified from wall to wall, shelves overloaded. Sonic and visual levels work at cross-purposes; hectic advertising form expresses the incoherence of the presentational space; the immanent singularity of networked entertainment rubs up against its potential dissolution.

Which is why the campaign van follows with the promise of replacement, as in replacing the representatives, a vague populistic call to bring clarity to hard-working American folk (a theme that will pick up the next time we hear the Walker voice, outside the airport). For now, though, the van exits its garage proscenium, shot frontally like a door-curtain raised onto the film's diegesis, and leads the camera along with it down the road to a recording studio. This opening is hyperconventional—a door opens onto the spectator, a vehicle moves toward the implied position of the spectator, a following shot pulls us slowly and gradually into the story world. It moves from closed stasis and enters the bumper-to-bumper traffic of Nashville and *Nashville*. It is *hyper*-conventional because it suggests (if not quite demands) that we recognize the convention as we see it. The Walker van and its acousmatic voice, not named as one of the film's twenty-four characters, establishes its narratological role. It *is* narration embedded within narrative, and it literally broadcasts its special role in the film to come—suturing narrational discourse to diegesis. Robert Niemi calls it, and the non-presence it paradoxically embodies, a "spectral transcendental signified."[7] It is the chariot that would redeem all of Nashville/*Nashville*'s fragments if it were ever to produce the messiah it promises. Ultimately, it serves a narrative desire: to only connect, to clarify, to reduce and replace, like Walker's campaign promise to "change our national anthem back to something people could understand." Whether it succeeds or fails at any of this is played out by the film's whole big network form.

No, Really Count 'Em

Flip to the front of a play and you will find a character list. The list ostensibly names the nodes in its character network, like the ingredients at the top of a recipe but without the amounts (it would be nice if, when reading *Hamlet* for the first time, we were told how many ounces of the prince we'll have to stomach). Expansive Russian novels, on the other hand, often lack paratextual character rundowns, and given my lack of facility with the culture's patronymics and diminutives I find it helpful to make them myself. That practice comes in handy here too. In no particular order, here are *Nashville*'s main players:

1. Haven Hamilton (played by Henry Gibson), a jingoistic country star in a Nudie suit; cuts a figure somewhere between Roy Acuff and Hank Snow. Knows who belongs in Nashville and who doesn't.
2. Opal (Geraldine Chaplin), a British documentarian who (says she) works for BBC Radio. Not exactly professional.
3. Lady Pearl (Barbara Baxley), Haven's paramour who manages a bluegrass club. Really misses the Kennedys.
4. Linnea Reese (Lily Tomlin), a gospel singer and mother to two deaf children/
5. Delbert Reese (Ned Beatty), Linnea's husband, Haven's attorney, organizer for the Walker campaign.
6. Barbara Jean (Ronee Blakley), a beloved country star in an ambiguously fragile state. Looks a bit like Loretta Lynn.

7. Connie White (Karen Black), Barbara Jean's top rival on the Nashville scene. Looks a bit like Tammy Wynette.
8. Tom Frank (Keith Carradine), one of the folk trio Bill, Mary, and Tom, and a solo playboy.
9. Tricycle Man (Jeff Goldblum), a silent presence who low-rides his three-wheel bike around town. Occasionally performs magic tricks.
10. Tommy Brown (Timothy Brown), one of the seemingly few Black singers to perform at Nashville's Grand Ole Opry. Looks a bit like Charley Pride.
11. L. A. Joan (Shelley Duvall), originally named Martha, has come to town to visit her aunt on her deathbed, but seems to do anything but. Primarily interested in getting close to famous people.
12. Barnett (Allen Garfield), Barbara Jean's husband and manager. Always a bit aggravated.
13. Sueleen Gay (Gwen Welles), aspiring country singer with neither talent nor self-awareness. "Can't sing a lick."
14. Wade Cooley (Robert DoQui), an ex-con who works with Sueleen at the airport restaurant and knows she has no talent. Drinks around town and seems to see through everyone else.
15. Pfc. Glenn Kelly (Scott Glenn), Vietnam veteran and Barbara Jean superfan. Doesn't say much; has probably seen some shit over there.
16. Kenny Frasier (David Hayward), a guy with a violin case. Seems like a perfectly nice mama's boy, at first.
17. Bill (Allan F. Nichols), the Bill from Bill, Mary, and Tom; married to Mary.
18. Mary (Christina Raines), the trio's lead vocalist, married to Bill but in love with Tom.
19. Norman (David Arkin), the folk trio's chauffeur. A bit of a *schlimazel*.
20. Mr. Green (Keenan Wynn), L. A. Joan/Martha's uncle, husband to Aunt Esther. Runs a boarding house in town.
21. Winifred (Barbara Harris), also known as Albuquerque, another aspiring country star. Avoids her husband as she searches out gigs.

22. John Triplette (Michael Murphy), consultant and organizer on the Walker campaign. Polished, manipulative, and definitely from California.
23. Star (Bert Remsen), Winifred's husband, straight out of the sticks.
24. Bud Hamilton (Dave Peel), Haven's son, graduate of Harvard Law, came back to Nashville to work for his father.
25. Hal Phillip Walker (voiced by Thomas Hal Phillips), an outsider presidential candidate not officially counted in the twenty-four, perhaps because he is never seen, only heard. Thinks Washington lawyers are the problem with America these days; wants to replace them.

Not bad as a simple character list goes. But in *Nashville*, thinking of characters as individuals can be misleading. In *Nashville*, that is, sacred American individualism is inherently misleading, a fantasy or fortress for cultural anxieties under perpetual siege. Once you see entertainment and politics as faces on a two-sided coin, you start to see doubles everywhere in this world. Here is one possible way to organize the ensemble as a collection of character pairs:

1. Haven and Tom: Toxically male stars with cynically duplicitous public personas. One lords at the nexus of Nashville's official culture, the other at the nexus of *Nashville*'s sexual circuit.
2. Opal and L. A. Joan: Outsiders wandering through Nashville with designs on cultural infiltration.
3. Lady Pearl and Triplette: Behind-the-scenes operatives or *éminence grise*. One a Nashville insider and the other a cultural outsider, their roles appear to flip as the film proceeds. One's political ideals have been dashed by present circumstances and a sense of American decline, the other embodies slick, Nixonian, media-savvy politics.
4. Barbara Jean and Linnea: Good-hearted, at times even angelic, women living with domineering men. One is

a superstar country music darling, the other fronts a gospel choir.
5. Delbert and Barnett: Heavy-set managerial men. One seems to barely acknowledge his wife's existence, the other never tires of reminding him of everything he does for her.
6. Walker and Tricycle Man: Roving vehicular figures making their ways around town. One is a voice without a face, the other is a face without a voice.
7. Albuquerque and Sueleen: Nashville ingénues similar in their naivete but far apart in terms of raw talent.
8. Tommy and Wade: Black men occupying very different positions in Nashville's white-dominated cultural spaces. One is accepted by the Haven Hamilton establishment, which leads the other to call him a race traitor (really, he calls him much worse).
9. Kelly and Kenny: Two loners. One follows Barbara Jean around town, the other drifts toward some invisible end.
10. Mr. Green and Star: Two men chasing younger women around town. One wants to corral his niece to his wife's bedside, the other chases after his runaway wife as she tries to make it out on her own.
11. Bill and Mary: Musical group members married to each other, not so happily.
12. Connie and Bud: A bit of a stretched pair, perhaps. The cute blondes? Connie could certainly have been productively paired with or against her rival Barbara Jean instead.

Left over: Norman. He wants to be a part of things, to guide the starstruck around town, but no one else seems willing to indulge. His whole affect is of the left out, the endlessly remaindered.

Frank Caso writes that "it is the characters' subtle complexities that lift the film beyond the simple Manicheanism with which it flirts."[8] The character pairs are real but provisional and revisable. Chauffeur Norman taps in as Tricycle Man's opposite number from time to time. Connie is Barbara Jean's rival and replacement (the Wynette to her Lynn), and Bud does project with Linnea a soft-spoken, sweet-hearted, second fiddle in the family affect—we have then a square arrangement with the blonde pair on one side and the brunettes on the other and diagonals connecting each corner. And pairs proliferate downward like fractals: Elliott Gould and Julie Christie both briefly appear, for example, playing themselves.

No reason to stop there, though. What if we introduce each character not as an individual or as part of a pair but as part of a cluster? Like a kaleidoscope that shakes its beads as it turns, the film's characters constantly assemble, shuffle, and reassemble. Here is a tentative, revisable, overlapping, and misleadingly simplified set of groupings:

1. Haven, Lady Pearl, Delbert, Bud—the country music scene's business class.
2. Walker PA, Triplette, Delbert, Haven—the Replacement Party's local cabal.
3. Haven, Barbara Jean, Connie, Tommy, Linnea, Bill/Mary/Tom, Albuquerque, Sueleen—a hierarchical spectrum of musicians and performers, of varying success and influence.
4. Lady Pearl, Delbert, Barnett, Wade, Pfc. Kelly, Norman, Mr. Green, Triplette, Star, Bud—helpers, organizers, spouses, second fiddles.
5. Walker PA., Opal, Tricycle Man, L. A. Joan, Tom, Pfc. Glenn, Kenny, Norman, Albuquerque—wanderers through the Nashville landscape, often observing and connecting otherwise distant characters.

Even organizing it this way reveals something about the film's character network. There is a hierarchical, pyramidal infrastructure supporting the flat, dispersed chaos of crisscrossing paths and plotlines. The public, celebrity representatives of Nashville culture and politics are relatively few, while the characters doing the unsung narrative labor, stitching the network together behind the scenes, make up a larger slice of the ensemble. This is something *Nashville* allows us to see, and we might argue that it is part of its networked politics to reveal *both* the social hierarchy *and* the way that hierarchy is sustained, through various asymmetries of major and minor characters. There is a class system, in other words, of *character*, which suggests without entirely reifying or simply presenting a political, economic, or cultural hierarchy. The problem with taking these groupings at face value, though, is that these clusters are porous. Like Tom sleeping around, the libido guiding *Nashville*'s character web is unrepentantly polyamorous. And yet, following along, we cannot entirely dispense with the structure of cluster formation. We must account for the cluster form as a narrative principle, the subtly stratified ensemble (except for rare but important exceptions) as the foundation of *Nashville*'s scenic structure.

We can group small clusters, for example, by the churches characters attend on Sunday:

1. Lady Pearl, Sueleen, Wade, and Star—Catholic.
2. Haven, Bud, Delbert (with his sons)— ambiguously Protestant.
3. Tommy (with his wife), Linnea—Black Baptist.
4. Barbara Jean, Barnett, Mr. Green, Pfc. Kelly— hospital chapel.

Or which music clubs they patronize, which vehicles they use to get around town, who appears with whom on stage or in conversation around tables.

In nearly every film with an identifiable narrative structure, we come to understand characters as existing in hierarchies— implicit rankings of importance which follows both their causal role in the story's development and what David Bordwell calls "the degree to which [characters'] narrative functions activate aspects of the person schema," traits, emotions, and thoughts irreducible to their basic motor impact on the action depicted.[9] We also compare characters according to "dimensions of personhood," an activity that is easier or more difficult to do depending on the number of characters we have to perceive, then consider. We can think about both character hierarchies of importance or centrality and webs of relation as matters of degree complexity based on how far the film departs from the simplest cases (where a small, single cluster of characters with starkly defined and mutually exclusive traits and goals interact within a relatively static environment). The more character traits, motivations, appearances, and narrative weights overlap, the closer we get to a network form, even if there is no obvious point at which a non-network turns into a network. How many grains of sand do you need before you call them all a pile?

Maybe what makes *Nashville* a true network film—and arguably *the* network film in the history of cinema—is less the number of characters or their degrees of overlap than it is the difficulty of distinguishing the narratable motivations they would each (in a different sort of film) singly possess. Classical Hollywood form demands clarity in the exposition of principal characters' goals and motivations. And clarity in turn usually demands viewer-facing presentation early in the film, the characters stepping through antechambers in the narrative discourse where they announce, or at least strongly imply, their basic desires, plans, and dilemmas. Such moments are analogues to conventional introductions of characters in realist novels, where narrators self-consciously paint their physical appearance, their dress, their distinctive characteristics, and even their distinguishing personality traits in words, stamping their entry tickets into the plot. Though character motivations may change for internal or external reasons—emotional self-development, say, or as the result of new information or unexpected events— viewers can at least track who they are and what they want across the span of the story's timeline. But films may cloud character transparency by delaying or eliding the revelation of their motivations. Or even, in rarer but not necessarily exceptional cases, never revealing them explicitly at all. The effect can be realistic, as when the reticence or passivity of a character feels more truly like people we would observe in our own lives—for how many people straightforwardly announce or display their long or medium-range intentions in non-intimate situations? It can also be formalistic and aesthetically challenging—is it not the basic compact of realistic narrative that narration be transparent about what's really "going on" with the characters we are asked to follow, judge, and (hopefully) care about? Is not some level of intimacy with and access to character excessive of "real-life" encounters (perhaps even the most intimate!) just the *sine qua non* of any narrative text?

But that is not the same thing as saying that we need to know everything, every character's psychological motivation, or that we even could. Much of life lacks adequate, properly overdetermining backstory or sufficient closure. Some network films do attempt intricate mechanisms of motivation and closure, as if trying to meet classical Hollywood narrative expectations at the end of a purposefully difficult narrative obstacle course. *Nashville* comes in at the other end of the spectrum. If there are story threads, they tangle up into a knotted mess. Characters drift, connect, disconnect, recombine, and drift again. Some clearly lack and want, like Sueleen, who on her own might have commanded a showbiz-style "star is born" pathway. Though what she lacks is not just fame and status but talent, and so she goes nowhere but to the bottom. Other characters go about their way without tipping us off as to what they are really up to. Like Tricycle Man, or Kenny and his mysterious violin case. Some merely exist to carry other folks around town, like Norman. In some cases, we learn their goals by the end of the film, but still lack clear understanding of their underlying reasons for acting. We may doubt that even they know why they do what they do.

"Invade My Picture"

The easiest, and therefore most misleading, way to diminish the complexity of Altman's filmmaking and Tewkesbury's screenwriting is to say they proceed without narrative structure.[10] Greil Marcus, in one of the harshest reviews of the film ever penned, sees the bad faith looseness of Altman's method everywhere: "Altman objectifies this vague feeling [of hopelessness or aimlessness] into argument by presenting an unmotivated and all but incomprehensible act of murder," and

> it is probably spoiling all the fun to point out that before a work can be convincing as a metaphor for something as big and complex as America . . . before it can function as anything so grand as a portrait of "our fall from grace," a book or movie must be convincing on the more basic, if seemingly tiresome level of play, character, motivation, and quotidian detail.[11]

For Marcus, the flatness of the vague ideas at the origin of large canvas works like *Nashville* and E. L. Doctorow's *Ragtime* correlate with a lack of control over the narrative basics. Fair or not, the fundamentals of narrative are the fundamentals. Recall, from the previous chapter, Kristin Thompson's account of classic Hollywood narrative form, structured around goal-oriented protagonists: four acts that together make a "unified narrative," where "a cause should lead to an effect and that effect in turn should become a cause for another effect, in an unbroken chain across the film."[12] Tewkesbury built her storyboard on totally different principles. She charted her scenes according to the variables of time and character, the former on her wall graph's y-axis and the latter along its x-axis. Her graph became a virtual, quantitative map of the spatio-temporal world of *Nashville*. Making a plot becomes an act of mathematical plotting, coordinating interactions as coordinates on a geometric plane. Tewkesbury complicated her initial plan by devoting yellow pieces of paper to each character, which she could, as Jan Stuart reports, "move around like flags on a war map."[13] While the war map would eventually have to become a script in pages, the film's narrative structure remains grounded throughout the production process in a large canvas or wide field of recombinatory interactions, better visualized as a multi-dimensional graph that reveals one of its surfaces at a time than as a line that rises and falls.

Now, it is not as if Altman's films dispense with all linear storylines or developments. In interviews, he has referred to certain characters as "clotheslines," spanning the length of a film, on which to hang incidents and scenes. They may not fit the Hollywood hero mold, and they might act more like bit parts than protagonists, but in following them throughout a movie we find them in close contact with most significant events that occur (even if they are not direct causal agents those events). They are agents of narration rather than plot. Indeed, clotheslines, if we look deeper into the metaphor, have neither personalities nor desires, but they do serve a function. The movement of the Walker van around town is one such clothesline in *Nashville*. It leads us into the recording studio at the film's open and shows up again outside the airport in the very next scene. Because the chronologies of the film's narration and plot parallel one another—we have no reason to believe, in other words, that we flash backward or forward in story time within or between scenes—the van's appearance at any time or location signifies, first, a spatial proximity between all characters in the story world. In *Nashville*, any character can reasonably appear in any scene. Their entrances are unremarkable, even probable. Whether the Walker campaign enters eye- or earshot is literally a matter of probability, since Altman teamed "Walker" (i.e., Phillips) with an organizer named Ron Hecht, equipped them with the van, set them up with a modest budget for stickers, signage, and apparel, handed them the film's shooting schedule, and told them "to invade [his] picture."[14] Walker's campaign, not just the van and its voice but the distribution of campaign swag throughout the world of the story, thus becomes a fundamentally probabilistic element that reveals the chanciness of the entire diegetic network. We see Walker's upstart presence spread like a virus through the town without ever seeing the man himself. The insurgent form of his insider–outsider presence in the film, to

FIGURE 3 *Walker invades the picture.*

which Altman cleverly gives an improvisatory rhythmic form by setting an initiative and letting the campaign do its thing, stitches *Nashville*'s Nashville together in guerilla fashion.

It may be the first we see and hear, but the Replacement Party van is not the only structural force that pulls heterogeneous elements into sprawling totality. What else generates the film's associations, metonymic relations, subliminal linkages? What else constitutes *Nashville*'s network form, and how does it reorient our attention to the film as it proceeds in narrational time?

Signal Switch

Network films can reveal something about narrative cinema in general: links between its units (shots, scenes, acts) are always mediated by form, even when that form is partially hidden by habits of viewing and the historical attainment of movie fluency. "All of us are deeply involved with politics whether we know it or not or like it or not." So the Walker van announces as it approaches an intersection. As it proceeds down the street, a martial drumbeat enters the audio mix. The traffic signal switches from red to green, and the van continues down the road, taking Walker's voice with it. We are sent onto another (sound)track, pulled to the side across a sound bridge by music coming from inside a recording studio (we will learn in a few seconds, at least, that it is the music being recorded in the studio). "That's politics"—the last proposition from the PA urges us not to let our ideological guard down as we are introduced via colonial drum rolls to Haven Hamilton recording his kitschily patriotic bicentennial battle hymn, "Two Hundred Years." The lyrics are not particularly profound, of course—"I pray my sons won't go to war, but if they must, they must. / I share our country's motto, and in God I place my trust. / We may have had our ups and downs, our times of trials and fears . . . / But we must be doin' something right to last two hundred years!" But the way the film sutures three signals together—the elementary cut from exterior to interior, the traffic light's switch, and the overlapping swerve in the soundtrack from campaign messaging to studio recording—establishes a just-off-balance overlap of perceptual levels, demanding a retraining of audience attention.

A relatively simple complex of audiovisual phenomena, the film's first cut provides a legend for the way the film is going to work. It also establishes the sort of viewer it has in mind or hopes to interact with—someone vigilant enough to perceive details compositionally decentered or backgrounded in a shot or mix, but open enough to cinema's diverse resources to be pulled across its internal thresholds, to be moved somewhere unexpected. It recruits curious tourists, eager for knowledge and information but without too many presuppositions about the town they wander through. Because *Nashville* is a film about a place rather than the place itself, spectators are obviously guided by a firmer hand than a travel guidebook's. Still, within the format boundaries of the feature film, Altman stretches attentional prerequisites. The film's syntax is not straightforwardly linear but contains links that cross medial thresholds. Meaningful relationships and narrative causes connect in abstract space, like a virtual network graph shifting in real time behind (or above, or beneath, or parallel to) the action we see and hear. David Bordwell calls these sorts of invisible connections "poetic linkages" because they are more "remote" and "fragile" than the "concrete" and "well-defined" links that count for a data scientist or social theorist studying networks.[15] When Walker says "That's politics" over his vehicle's PA system, he announces the tenor that will shortly be matched by the metaphorical vehicle pulsing through Haven Hamilton's studio microphone—politics is happening here, in the music, and even in the Nudie-suit figure cut by the establishment country star who demands insider musicians only, kicking outsiders like Opal out of the room, ordering Frog the session pianist (played by Richard Baskin, the film's music director and, in an Altmanesque wink, cowriter with Gibson of the very song they are failing to record together) to cut his hippie hair. Haven struggles and ultimately fails to keep foreigners, women, hippies, and—as we will see in the next studio room over—Blacks out of the picture. So then who, we wonder, are Walker's "fellow taxpayers and stockholders in America"? Like frequencies interacting in the space between sources, *Nashville*'s syntactical links are relations of resonance.

"Resonance" might be a strange term of art to some who, like Robin Wood writing in the year of *Nashville*'s release, emphasize Altman's "centrality" to American cinema as an expressive linchpin for a "growing sense of disorientation and confusion of values."[16] But if resonance occurs when an acoustic system amplifies a sound ringing out at certain frequencies, we might sharpen comments like Wood's by saying that Altman films disperse and distribute viewer (and listener) attention broadly among its links—its multiple character and plot pathways, the intra-scene stylistic flattening that confuses sensory registers and widens its ambience to broaden the number of perceivable signals we must try to be aware of at any moment—so as to occasionally (but *only* occasionally) heighten the energies and information vibrating subliminally through the network. Robert Self analyzes Altman's oeuvre as a serial exercise in articulating "subliminal reality," a project Altman advocates: "I'm not so much interested with a good yarn as I am [with] atmosphere. . . . I'm more interested in the subliminal reality. I'm more interested in touching people on an unconscious basis to where they sense something rather than intellectually know or agree to something."[17] Self calls Altman's aesthetic anti-classical insofar as classical Hollywood plotting "reflects an ideological and psychological realm of human separation and desire . . . that the narrative seeks to order and regulate, to realize and unify through the fantasy of control."[18] Subliminal reality exists beyond narrational control, as a "more diffuse, splintered, ambiguous field of knowledge" where "human behavior transcends intelligible motivation, where meaning outstrips consciousness." Self does not define Altman's anti-classical filmmaking as network cinema, but the ingredients are all there. And what's more, the "diffuse, splintered, ambiguous field of knowledge" Altman's films create need not only be seen as alienating or confusing, since it is ultimately a field of *knowledge*. It is just that the formal means of producing that knowledge challenge the "easy control" techniques of traditional filmic structure—all those things that help deliver cinema's busy fields of stimulus in easy-to-read packaging—like continuity editing, well-focused visual and auditory *Gestalten*, informative blocking patterns, linear rise-and-fall plotting, or protagonist- and antagonist-centered character systems.

Crafting atmosphere, as Altman tries to do, sounds oxymoronic. It is hard enough to read the feeling in a room, let alone make that feeling appear. Is it possible to create and communicate that which, almost by definition, eludes conscious control? Atmospheres are fundamentally relational. They cannot be localized to a point, though they might fill an abstract container—as Dora Zhang puts it, atmosphere as a concept "names, in effect, the spatialization of relationality."[19] It names the subliminal affective corollary to active networks, large and small. Sensing an atmosphere means discerning the emergence of a constellation, a fragile, gossamer web of bodies, feelings, intentions, and shared, implicit knowledge.

Nashville networks atmosphere, in part, through its famous sonic texture, which I will return to and discuss at some length. But also through overlaps established by the film's peculiar causal structures (on a macro level) and its focal techniques (which show or practice its relational principles at the micro). Altman's style sits somewhere around the apex of New Hollywood-era scan-and-reveal approach to profilmic subject matter, where cameras search visual fields for details to select and focalize.[20] Technically, this cinematographic method solicits pans (the scanning function) and zooms (the selecting function) across and into relatively long takes. Altman is particularly well known for his slow "creeping zooms." Sometimes they're called, quite appropriately, "subliminal zooms."[21] If Altman's zooms are subliminal, it is because they direct our attention unobtrusively. In an information-rich cinematographic field, they direct attentional movement, as Mark Minett puts it, "from a nondirected scanning of the image to a directed approach, with the direction provided by the zoom-in."[22] The creeping zooms are thus minimally self-conscious, evincing a narrational impulse that disguises itself, or makes itself *feel* unconscious, even as it ultimately succeeds in directing our conscious attention to specificities in the master shot—a quiet conversation unfolding in the deep field, a pregnant glance on one side of the frame, someone leaving out a back door with someone else they should not be leaving with. John Belton and Lyle Tector take this zoom subliminality to dissolve any "notion of a discrete narrator," since it is "consecrated to exploring the essential life-and-energy system of the world under scrutiny," as if all camera movement and focalizing in an Altman film is a symptom of the corresponding story world's vital relations.[23] We may take this point figuratively and acknowledge that the pan and zoom method supports the improvisatory chanciness of scenes in *Nashville* and other Altman pictures, rendering it intelligible and thereby establishing its basic, kinetic visual form.

But the camera does not often pan, select, and creep in on individual characters in *Nashville* as a means of revealing them or their previously overlooked salience in the visual field. Indeed, what Minett calls the "attentional zoom" is a much rarer technique, in the film and in Altman's oeuvre, than the criticism suggests. Tricycle Man is often tracked via zoom, as Richard Jameson notes: "His thoughtless mobility is sufficient to glide us into terrain we identify as our next scene, or up to a character we've been wondering about since he/she last passed through the frame. Altman pans and zooms not only with the man and his vehicle but also along the vectors so forcefully described and anticipated by the motion and the very chape of the machine."[24] Minett categorizes this use of the zoom the "reframing zoom," which maintains the structural value of moving figures within the scene or allows one figure to pass the compositional baton to another.[25]

An easy example (at least on screen), which falls under both "reframing" and "attentional" categories, is Tricycle Man's arrival at the airport. We cut from the slightest of leftward pans on the airfield to a spot across from the arrivals curb, immediately panning back to the left as the stationary camera follows the Tricycle Man (who in turn is followed by Walker's van, not always in frame but constantly heard). Within the frame of the airfield shot, a small cluster of Barbara Jean's welcome party (including Barnett) is tracked across a small waiting plaza by a news camera's own rightward pan, and the brief pan that ends the shot takes over from the camera inside the scene, as if it served as another point of Channel 2's visual coverage. The cut from the pan late in the previous shot, stitched into the path of the walking procession and its inner-diegetic media coverage, generates a sense of cinematographic momentum, as if the camera's movement kicks us from one location to the next, covering over the cut's seams. We follow the Tricycle Man's arrival until he parks his bike frame left, and for a split second we have a planimetric tableau, broken up formally by the airport's stanchions, with Walker's van momentarily in the center of the shot and Norman standing by his parked vehicle on the right. Once the van passes, its PA delivery still in earshot, Tricycle Man gets up and walks back to the right, and the camera pans back with him and creeps in, right up until he passes Norman (signaling to him ambiguously with a magician's silk scarves) and exits the frame. At that point, the camera ends its pan but continues to zoom in on Norman, who is now dead center in the frame. After a confused pause, Norman turns to follow Tricycle Man with an off-frame look. Norman's following glance pulls our attention back to the right, and we cut back to the airfield only to pan and follow a jet on the tarmac, once again from right to left. A reframing cut pulls us back, where Channel 2's reporter addresses us directly as if, once again, we were looking through the eye of a news camera, while Barbara Jean's plane continues to taxi in the background. There is nothing about this sequence that will pull you from your seat; Altman's less common, more stylized attentional zooms very well might. But the more ubiquitous camera movement that bridges shots, locations, and character crossings traces the pathways—walking, driving, speaking, looking, attending—that network those characters in space and time, primarily through compositional means.

As Altman's camera stitches itself into the fabric of the unfolding media coverage, it achieves an added layer of narrational self-consciousness. Sometimes our attention is directed through the official channels of *Nashville*'s Public Relations machine. Sometimes it wanders around

FIGURE 4 *Airport, curbside.*

its periphery. But since camera movement and sound bridge the two across scenic intercuts, we see both nesting within a greater totality. Even if they feel haphazard, improvisatory, and chancy, Altman's audiovisual relationships remain highly motivated. I want to call that motivation, that formal-stylistic desire, "networking." *Nashville*, that is, expresses a *desire to network*. In the term's more vulgar, banal meaning, that's what *Nashville*'s aspirational characters try to do—Opal, Sueleen, Albuquerque, Triplette, Norman, L. A. Joan are networking. But as a *narrational* mode, networking at both its most obvious and most subliminal transcends causes set in motion by individual character motivations. Instead, *Nashville*'s multi-track pathways, many of which are primarily sensory, work by being immanent to a larger-scale form, of the virtual network of interrelations whose canvas is too large for the screen. This virtual network, unframeable and unseeable, animates the creeping zooms, the following pans, the sound bridges, the choreography. The film's signal switches are surface effects of a subliminal depth, constantly shuffling, beneath whatever we are given to see or hear. *Nashville* outsources or redistributes causal significance beyond traditional character motivations, which are not eliminated but *symptomatized*, expressed without being directly represented in the network's links, which seek adequate cinematic syntax and form.

"Welcome to Nashville"

Nashville is chockablock with puns that cross medial thresholds. When Haven tells Frog to get his hair cut, that he "don't belong in Nashville," we guess that the bored pianist likely won't follow the direction. But, in an admixture of obedience and defiance, the film cuts hard to the city's airfield, to its "Welcome to Nashville" sign prominently displayed on the signal tower. The sign is a two-way signal of its own, welcoming tourists, visitors, and musicians to the city in the story world even as it provides yet another introduction to the film itself. At the airport, we will encounter nearly all the significant characters we have not yet had the pleasure of meeting. But there is no valet holding our sign ("Viewer" or "Spectator"), waiting to whisk us out of the crowd and take us downtown. Instead, we are left to get lost in all the hubbub.

The airport scene is the point in the growth of *Nashville*'s network form when it achieves connectivity, gains what network theorists call a giant component (a section of a network graph that contains a large percentage of that network's vertices). It also makes for a good microcosm, like a tabletop version of the bigger thing. Airports are made of runways, terminals, and lounges. The last is an infrastructural component just like the others, and here we approach the truth of this scene—it is one big character lounge. Aaron Kunin asks, in a recent study of character form, "What happens when characters get together?"[26] Referencing Doug Allen's comic strip *Steven*, Kunin theorizes a Characters Lounge, an off-frame, virtual green room where characters wait to enter or re-enter a plot. Earlier in this book I mentioned Alex Woloch's related notion of character systems, which take shape and structure over the temporal course of a narrative, apportioning attention, power, and causal influence in a finite, zero-sum character space. In *Nashville*, the airport scene self-consciously establishes that virtual space, which was already marked (in miniature) as contested and regulated in the studio scene. Now it expands, perhaps too much for domineering folks like Haven Hamilton to control.

The official reason for the scene, what makes it more than your average day at the airport, is Barbara Jean's return to town from the Baltimore Burn Center (as we hear from Channel 2's Bill Jenkins, an explanation that we slowly come to doubt as a reliable backstory). As part of the film's meta-plot, it is the first scene designed to get almost all of the principal characters together, and is the convenient prelude to the traffic jam that will clinch the first complete character nexus. What was then called Berry Field was certainly no O'Hare, but in the world of *Nashville*, it is a veritable hub. As a critical mass of players enter the film—from the air, from the parking lot, through jet bridges, and in the process of simply doing their jobs—a vague idea of social connection (the populist desires streaming through Walker's PA system, the patriotic rhetoric of Haven's recording) materializes. As a dense crowd of fans await and then react to Barbara Jean's return, Altman's roving camera picks out character vertices from the throng. For the first time in the film, we get a sense of fully circumambient space rather than a spatial layout organized by a line of vehicular progress or an adversarial, oppositional structure.

As a matter of narrative structure, the scene generates an expectation of concentrated exposition. Welcome to *Nashville*—here are the prime players, all at once, and everything you need to know to understand who they are and what they want. Concentrated exposition need not come at the beginning of a narrative's discourse (it can be delayed in the syuzhet rather than propaedeutic), though it typically does. Meir Sternberg, using Jane Austen's *Emma* as a primary example, defines exposition by the way it is "marked off from the action proper," creating a telescopic "disparity in time-ratios" between the action presented directly through exposition and the action that directly follows.[27] Concentrated exposition generalizes, both temporally and spatially. It self-consciously marks a difference between how things have been and how they might now change (in *Emma*, as in many protagonist-driven novels, marking a new era in the titular character's personal history, one of intense self-reflection, maturity, and eventually, real love). The narrator thereby signals boundaries around the primary plotline.

The means by which this kind of exposition is delivered in fiction versus film differ, of course. But in both cases, with concentrated exposition all the self-consciousness is on the side of the narrator/narration. The information is clearly, sometimes too clearly, addressed to the reader/viewer; all expository narration is, of course, but the more it is stacked up at once the more it is packaged as general knowledge rather than as singular events taking place. In what Chatman calls distributed exposition, information is braided throughout the text's emplotment, dispersed to be gleaned along the way. It can be disclosed through devices like flashback or come to us through dialogue or narrated memory. Storytellers thereby "exploit the flexibility of their medium—notably the possibility of constructing an innumerable number of sujets out of the same fabula—to open expositional gaps by artificially deforming the chronological sequence."[28] In other words, they open, manipulate, and fill gaps in the story world chronology to generate unknowingness, surprise, and the event of coming to know either along with, ahead of, or behind characters' own knowledge of their situations. Narrators and narrative devices open and restrict the range of our knowledge too, when we do have it. So what about *Nashville*? How does it work, as a matter of narratological exposition?

Altman's films generally provide far less overt exposition than the norm and a maximal amount of expository distribution. The information that adequately backs the motivations and stories of the people we (often struggle to) track from scene to scene is rarely concentrated. Which does not mean it's totally absent. But it comes to us indirectly, slantwise, circuitously. Exposition, we might say, is *networked*. The backstory we most ache to know as the airport scene develops is what really happened to Barbara Jean. This narrational exposition is not exactly delayed, since it is never really delivered at all, at least not directly. And who is Pfc. Kelly, really, and why is he so devoted to Barbara Jean? The airport scene provokes our curiosity about characters who disembark and enter the story without exposition beyond whatever is implied in their dress and speech style. Our expectations about where each are going are unspecific. We are forced into limiting our large-scale narrative expectations in favor of episodic ones. Martha is supposed to visit her dying aunt, but clearly prefers to wander off (in the guise of her preferred *nom de groupie*, L. A. Joan), away from her official chaperone Mr. Green, in search of someone or something else. Sueleen, meanwhile, who we meet at the airport soda fountain, has a more explicit narrative path governed by an articulable desire for stardom, but we immediately gather that her dream may never even get off the ground.

It might seem counterintuitive to argue that network narratives demand narrational compression. But there are compensatory pressures unleashed by a network's inherent sprawl, including the need to crop the totality within spatial, temporal, or conceptual frames. As more characters arrive at Berry Field, the scarcity of screen time becomes more of a problem and the narrational system becomes noisier and noisier. The frames, in other words, need to be cut snugger. That there are several now-conventional means of doing so, as discussed in the previous chapter, is evidence that compressing a network's inherent expansive tendency is the form's primary structural problem. Network films are fueled by connection but risk breaking down when their engines flood, on entropic overload. Anti-democratic concerns to this effect stretch at least as far back, in America, to the framers of the United States Constitution, whose formal problem was how to adequately "frame" a republic that broke down due to legal fragmentation under the previous Articles of Confederation. Much of US legal history departs from a founding contradiction between political centralization (federalism) and regionalism (anti-federalism). Telling stories about a culture or society, not to mention a nation, demands expressing one system in the terms of another, carrying real relations and contradictions over into another medial form, reducing them in the process without losing too many of their essential properties.

If that sounds somehow above the chaotic energy of *Nashville*'s airport scene and subsequent pileup (of which more in just a minute), let me try to assure you why it's not. Woloch traces what he calls "an asymmetric structure of characterization—in which many are represented but attention flows toward a delimited center" to social stratification, registering (in his study, in the novel form) "the competing pull of inequality and democracy" in bourgeois realist narrative works.[29] Asymmetric character systems, "which rounds out one or several characters while flattening, and distorting, a manifold assortment of characters" both reflects real social hierarchies and inequity and generates the claims of minor characters on our attention.[30] Competing forces of hierarchy and democracy, inequity and equity, are inflected into textual metanarratives. In Woloch's bravura reading of Jane Austen's *Pride and Prejudice*, social disequilibrium—the pressures on families to single out specific daughters as particularly marriageable, given the scarcity of wealthy bachelors in their local communities—produces out of an initially flat network of sisters and young women a true protagonist whose inner life exceeds that of every other character in the novel: Elizabeth Bennet, of course.[31] Far from *Nashville* and 1970s America, to be sure, but it's the same type of hydraulic pressure, percolating up from other social contexts, that generates the specific topologies of character networks that govern other narrative texts, including those we find throughout the history of twentieth-century cinema. We are simply talking about the difference between true and relative protagonism and flatter ensembles, which reach their apex in network narratives.

The flatter the ensemble, the more broadly characters are networked, the more eccentric those characters become. This, I claim, is definitional. It is the character side of the space-time compression—the reduction to bounded location or to shorter time units, or both—network narratives are pressured into by practical necessity. Altman's films embrace this principle rather than try to resist it. Even if networked character systems flatten the difference between major and minor characters, members of an ensemble take on some of the characteristics of minorness in protagonist-driven narratives, including eccentricity. Character is distorted by the compression demanded by putting the network into a frame smaller than it wants to be in. And Altman's zooms and camera movements are a mediated, stylistic expression of eccentricity, demanded by the attentional sprawl of the larger canvas. The camera's treatment of Martha/L. A. Joan upon her arrival in the terminal is a case in point. Dressed in colorful platform shoes and knee socks, hot pants, bandeau top, and beret, we first see her off in the middle distance on the right side of the frame as Triplette and Delbert meet in the center-left foreground. A slow creeping zoom pulls us ever so slightly toward the men as they greet each other awkwardly and walk off frame together, at which point the camera pans to the right to bring L. A. Joan briefly to the center of our attention before a cut. When we return to Joan after a brief airfield sequence, Mr. Green is in the middle of greeting her; she tells him that she's changed her name. When Tom walks past them, accompanied by three stewardesses, the camera follows the group to the camera's left. Joan leaves her uncle behind and follows Tom, asking him to sign a record. The sequence is subtle in every regard except for its representation of Joan—her outfit, her restlessness, her single-minded drive to attach herself to nothing and nobody but celebrities. A character otherwise in the middle ground, in Nashville supposedly to visit her dying aunt, ingratiates herself into the nexus of music, politics, and sex. If she is a cipher or caricature, that seems to be precisely the point here. And the way she is framed and tracked—as an eccentric detail in a scene (and *scene*) otherwise not about her, as a gravitational node or magnet pulling us just marginally toward the pivots of *Nashville*'s cultural ensemble—formalizes and stylizes the way networks establish and reconstruct centers and peripheries. *This*, the camera tells us, is what it's like to join a culture, to push your way in from the outside. This is what it looks like, at least.

L. A. Joan's drift away from the ostensible aim of her visit, toward the first person she notices from the cover of a vinyl album, keys in miniature the oblique, sideways, only partially directed vectors of network character nodes. Mr. Green's form of minor characterization is less eccentricity than the tender simplicity of a blocked aim—first he wants to bring his niece to his wife's deathbed, then he just wants to mourn. His tragedy is to be drawn into *Nashville* in the first place. He wants to fulfill the simplest domestic task, one worthy of narrativization but only in another type of film (like a quiet, pensive art film

FIGURE 5 *L. A. Joan's arrival.*

or a popular melodrama). The network form and its corollary in aimless 1970s star-chasing music fandom pushes him to its outskirts, the boarding house that functions as a character lounge for other peripheral characters. At the airport, we see Joan work her way into a circuitous character conveyor belt, into the form of circuitous drift, where an eccentric without the psychological fullness of a conventional protagonist thrives. Her uncle is left to pick up the bags. This little sequence is a microcosmic fractal piece of a hyper-realized world of comings and goings, connections and separations. Of little moment, it is the kind of precious, unglossable nexus of social layering out of which (much) larger worlds emerge.

Traffic Jam

"Who do you think is running Congress? Farmers? Engineers? Teachers? Businessmen? No, my friends, Congress is run by lawyers. A lawyer is trained for two things: to clarify and confuse." As we pick up Walker's PA voice outside the airport terminal, four small character groups shuffle around and find their cars, parked adjacently in a row. L. A. Joan and Mr. Green find their Nash; Triplette and Delbert a Cadillac;

Sueleen and Wade a busted-up pickup; and Tom a flower-powered Volkswagen Beetle stuffed with stewardesses, leaving Bill, Mary, and their chauffeur Norman to pass a set of keys around until they find the right one (the folk group's 3-and-1 fault line marking an asymmetrical exception in the scene's character groupings). As the cars start backing out of their spaces simultaneously, a Scruggs-style banjo tune enters the mix. It does not take a prey of lawyers for confusion to set in. What we see in this scene is the meta-formal result of a single camera's attempt to follow multiple protagonists in concert. Each parking space is like a slot from which a character group's story should take off in earnest, accelerating down a road we can follow at the proper narrational distance. But there can be no straight(forward) narrative progress when we try to take in all paths at once, only cognitive gridlock. The closer each character's narrative bumper comes to any other's, the less clarity we can get from that character articulated as an individual, with their own unique drives, desires, plans, and pathways.

There is only one narrow exit from the airport parking lot, regulated by a single confused parking arm. As the cars and vans pass through the one-lane exit the arm (whether automated or controlled by an attendant, we cannot see) hesitantly lowers but cannot stop any of the vehicles from following each other on their bumpers. Eventually, a tourist bus blows right through it. This is not a film where bottlenecks are easily sorted. *Nashville* drops a couch on the freeway of cinema history, setting a generic pileup in motion—as Bordwell puts it, "the most common chance-based convergence, as conventional as a Main Street shootout in a Western, is the traffic accident."[32] Here the conceit builds the network in a plausible, narratively efficient way. Degrees of separation compress into a bumper-to-bumper nexus; distributed plot pathways intersect, get knotted up, and slowly disentangle. If the airport scene acquires a giant component of character connectivity, the traffic jam that follows is the first where every major character in the film collides. It says a lot about where the major collision happens in the course of a network narrative: at the beginning, at the very end, at the plot's dramatic climax? Is it subordinated to the logic of the fabula or syuzhet? Does it set a web of interactions in motion, or serve as their culmination? In *Nashville*, though, the pileup and resulting gridlock is more ambient and ecological than propulsive and culminative.

The difference is best articulated by Opal, thinking like a foreign correspondent: "It's America. All those cars smashing into each other, and all those mangled corpses." Which is not just an exaggeration, but a fantasy. America is a culture of crowds, of commodified collectivity. The spectacle of groupthink. Even a school bus skids out, though no children appear to have been harmed in the making of the mass fender bender (which, surprisingly enough for an intricately choreographed sequence in an Altman film, took only one take). Typically, traffic accidents in network films are life-changing events. *There Were Days…and Moons* (1990), *Amores perros* (2000), *Changing Lanes* (2002), *11:14* (2003), *Hard Luck Hero* (2003), and (of course) *Crash* (2004) are just a few of the notable examples where car crashes suture the chanciness of networked life to the overdetermined, even fateful significance of the billiard ball collisions that characterize our lives when told as stories. In *Nashville*, though, the pileup stalls the story's forward propulsion rather than jump-starting it or sending

FIGURE 6 *Character gridlock.*

everyone down a vertiginous and theatrically violent path. It's true to life, we might say, in that it showcases intersecting lives at glancing blows rather than head-on smash-up.

The result of the pileup is thus leisurely circulation, not spectacle. Opal's morbid fascination is with violence and collision as fantasy object. But the crash is a narrative deflation. It retards plot progression, as if to burrow us deeper into the specific type of film *Nashville* is. Each automobile carries a character, or a character pair, or a small group that seem to belong together as a narrative unit—Barbara Jean in her ambulance, Kenny all alone in a green Chevy, Joan and her uncle fiddling with the radio, Star and Albuquerque in their red pickup, Triplette and Del sizing each other up by talking politics, Tom with his stewardesses, Haven and his family highly visible in their Jeep convertible, Tommy and his all-Black entourage cooped up in a tour bus (where they will be joined by Opal, crossing over a threshold the Americans in the scene will not). Their forward trajectories stalled, characters converse through windows or get out of their vehicles to set different, more horizontal, less propulsive side routes through the story world in motion. Just a bit later a separate, minor two-car crash offers a microscopic, scaled-down version of the larger network interaction of the pileup and its aftermath, offering the seeds of a narratological distinction between giant components and head-on antagonistic impact. The next morning, Albuquerque wakes up in the backseat of a car, parked at the intersection of Routes 10 and 40, beneath a Walker campaign flyer used as a blanket. Walker's voice bleats ironic internal narration: "We have some problems that money alone won't solve." Two identifiable vehicles cross on the state road: Tricycle Man's tricycle and Star's red pickup. Albuquerque then walks aimlessly across the street, digging through her bag. Behind her, two cars collide, though she does not notice and keeps walking toward the camera without turning. Both drivers get out of their cars, argue, and begin to fight as Albuquerque proceeds off-screen and two Walker volunteers take the opportunity to plant campaign stickers on each car's bumper.

When the unnamed volunteers plant WALKER FOR PRESIDENT on the unnamed combatants' cars, it is like one movie grabbing a little corner of another movie for its own. Those guys present us briefly with a glimpse of another storyline, curtailed so that we can walk on down toward the gas station restroom with Albuquerque and on down the road with the Walker van, its monologue continuing audibly without gaps across the visual cut, to Kenny, who crosses the van's path as the camera now follows him up to Mr. Green sitting on his front porch. Who knows how the scuffle ends? It doesn't matter because that's exactly the kind of tangential narrative conflict *Nashville* renounces. Their adjacent world, of a chance collision turning into full-blown agon, is the product of *Nashville*'s circumambient network but not the kind of causal link that generates its forward momentum. Why does one kind of traffic accident gather the film's characters while another more straightforwardly dramatic one barely registers as a plot point? Because the first does not make a dent in any of the vehicles while the second does. This is Altman's radical gambit: our lives are filled with causal overdeterminations and invisible influences, and more seldomly traumatic blow-ups. But the most significant causal forces, because much harder to recognize and thus possibly resist, make scrapes rather than dents. They pull us into orbits, like weak but effective magnets, rather than complete wrecks. They constellate collectives rather than one-on-one antagonisms, making us less protagonists in our special stories than members of an ensemble that keeps growing as we keep going. Until, of course, that rare moment when the event we've been slowly drifting toward, maybe even pretending not to notice as it approaches, arrives. But by then it is no longer only chance.

Figure Missing

Surely my readers expect, sooner rather than later, a comprehensive and visually elegant network diagram connecting all of *Nashville*'s characters (nodes) in a web of interactions (links). Then we can see which characters are central, and which are more peripheral. Who knows whom and who connects what to what. What degrees of connectivity structure the temporal unfolding of the film's actions and conflicts, its group dynamics. A little extra interpretation of the data can tell us why such a diagram emerged as a product of the neoliberal 1970s, or just the New Hollywood 1970s.

Sorry to disappoint. Here is why I am not including a social network diagram of the film, despite having spent hours coding the metadata. For one, *Nashville* is *too much of a network*, too noisy, to get much interpretive value from a map of its nodes and links. Which does not mean it is random; far from it. But still, the impossible act of trying to graph the film's network reveals the significance of its noise and its immanent hierarchies, the way it fails to be a random network of truly democratic relationality. Which is precisely the film's true politics: by creating a subliminal contradiction between the populism espoused by Walker's monologue and the organization of its characters into more and less powerful story nodes, *Nashville* challenges the hypnotic rhetoric of republican spectacle, the fantasy of liberatory collapse between popular entertainment and electoral politics. *Nashville*'s network as narrative cannot be adequately understood as a sum of its characters and their interactions. Instead, we must be open to the even deeper entanglement of its nodes as a temporal process that magnetizes undemocratic arrangements of power and influence.

The problems one faces when attempting to graph *Nashville* are initially methodological, though the methodological deadlocks ultimately serve a network reading by disclosing the formal entanglements that ground and reinforce the film's complexity. There are basic, non-trivial interpretive questions one must answer before (1) picking what counts as a scene or a unit of interaction; (2) determining whether a character "appears" in it, is adequately "present," or socially involved; (3) how and whether to link characters based on dialogue, shot appearance, or proximity; (4) how to establish direction of interaction, or the weight of an interaction/connection within a scene or across shots; and (5) how or whether to establish boundaries between the main twenty-five and minor characters outside the ensemble. Even these five tasks depend in turn on a deeper assumption: that the nodes of the network we want to quantify are characters and not some other relevant category, like locations (Bordwell does just this in his brief reading of *Nashville* in *Poetics of Cinema*, at one point defining the film's nodes as its sites of convergence, which range from large to midsize to small depending on how many characters occupy a scene together. In this case, nodes are places in the story world and links are established by the characters who appear in them. We can imagine a graph that shows how each place— the Opry, the airport, the Walker rally, the various music clubs, homes and studios and hotel rooms and the weirder corners of the town—connects to others by virtue of shared visitors and occupants. What a strange version of the narrative seems to emerge in this case! But only one of many). How one decides how to name and make the categories of metadata in the first place, their basic parameters, alters one's experience of the film's formal capacities. The linearity of a printable network graph (or even a series of printable graphs) would be as reductive as describing the film's narrative discourse linearly. Static network graphs can still be quite useful, just also highly provisional and as interpretation-laden (especially regarding the formal units in question) as any of the qualitative readings one might provide. *Nashville*, more than most texts one might quantify and map as a network, puts its roadblocks up, and *that is precisely what makes it such a good example of a network narrative.*

What counts as a single scene? *Nashville* regularly intercuts two (and occasionally more) locations, two scenes within a scene, connected speculatively through editing but each diegetically self-contained. The early scene at the recording studio (which I will return to yet again), split between Studios A and B, sets a key for the rest of the film's pairings and parallels, showing us how to think about their dialectical relationship, as an identity and a difference. The film often juxtaposes two scenes at competing music venues, each with a cluster of characters who come together through happenstance. There is nothing unusual in network films about cross-cutting between locations, but typically the complexity is paid for by a correspondingly clear difference between parallel threads. Altman's *Short Cuts*, arguably his most coherent thread-structure network, works by clearly demarcating locations and putting small character clusters into clear relief. The threads, in other words, are made visible even as small worlds interconnect through the mediation of specific individuals, the friends-of-friends, and happenstance collisions, like the central tragic moment where Doreen (played by *Nashville*'s own Lily Tomlin) hits Howard and Anne's young son with her car, though she never comes into direct contact with either of them. Evan Smith describes thread structures as actually featuring "several bona fide protagonists, each the hero in his or her own story," so that while these mini-protagonists' parallel (and inevitably truncated) journeys intersect and tie themselves into occasional knots, their individual goals and desires are still clearly marked off from the others'.[33] A heavily signposted narrative discourse usually accompanies threaded stories: we can easily imagine obtrusive section titles (like chapter headings in a novel) that name their characterological focus and cleanly identify shifts from one thread to another. In *Nashville*, by contrast, the rotating clusters of characters are far more chaotic, and the parallel crosscuts often conceal clear markers in the mises en scène, demanding that we focus our attention as much on large canvas oppositions and relations as on who is sitting next to whom at any given moment. Or who is speaking to whom, since speech is one and only one member of the film's sound system, often unprivileged.

Altman even suggests, in an interview with David Thompson, that the network constructed in his films is not just an effect or a result but a *tool*. It gives the filmmaker material to cut to. "If two actors are really happy with a scene and say they really want to do it, and we shoot a six-minute scene, and they're happy they have put a continuity into that, as long as I have something to cut away to, *an escape hatch*, I can get out of it and come back where I want to. And you don't need as much information as you're given in most films. If you're given all the information, you don't have anything to do yourself."[34]

Altman is responding to a question about *Short Cuts*, not *Nashville*, but the latter is the better example of the escape hatch principle. In the former, the "thread" film, storyline strands are visible or easily schematized, for the most part unproblematically diagrammable. Even as the threads cross and interweave, they are hardly chaotic, retaining their singularities or small ensemble forms even as they tangle. Whereas in *Nashville*, large, less-differentiated masses of characters gather in scenes and locations—at the studio, the airport, on the freeway, at concerts, benefits, lounges, and clubs, at church, at rallies. They break off for rendezvous and side conversations, only to recirculate through a sea of noise. There was so much material and so much character circulation that assistant director Alan Rudolph suggested making two movies out of it, and Altman and Rudolph even pitched the idea of a *Nashville Red* and *Nashville Blue*, each a reversal of the other where the same scenes would be encountered from different focal points, alternate groups of characters emphasized and de-emphasized in a figure-ground *Gestalt* switch.[35] The answer from the producers was no. But the idea was a reasonable response—reasonable for the filmmakers, I mean, not the money guys—to the kind of composition by field they were undertaking. It was an admission that the film did not (for better or worse, depending on one's taste) channel its characters into well-dug narrative grooves marked with plainly visible signage.

And not only that. In *Nashville*, characters shed their skins and circulate in doubly mediated forms, like Platonic copies-of-copies. Which is essential to the character system of a film in which entertainment and political industries churn through image distribution. Characters, in other words, *are* small networks within wider ones. Who, for instance, is Connie

White? Most of the film's characters appear to have inner lives, though each is left completely up to interpretation. Connie does not seem to have one, a condition suggested upon her introduction in the form of a poster image. Her posters, in fact, get almost as much face time as her actual face. The only major character who does not appear in or around the airport in the flesh, Connie's introduction comes via poster pinned to the side of the terminal music stand with, as Tewkesbury's script puts it, "a Hal Phillip Walker sticker attached to her bosom." Even her name tag points to someone other than herself! "Wait a minute," Bill says. "Hal Phillip Walker looks exactly like Connie White." And Connie's primary role in the film is to be a replacement for someone else: Barbara Jean (as Haven tells Triplette, "Connie White and Barbara Jean never appear on the same stage together. Connie might replace Barbara, but that's it"). She is the empty space in the character network that literalizes the shallow truth of characterization in *Nashville*: it depends at all moments on its external relations, which are unfixed and unstable. "I want you to study real hard," Connie tells the children in the Opry audience, "because just remember any one of you can grow up to the be the president." Not just a cliché but one dependent on the idea of fulfilling a role, the empty one at the center of the nation, the one we never see filled in the film because we never see Walker the candidate (the one who, more obviously than Connie, activates the force of "replacement" as an open and endless process).

White continues to be a force for undermining character as a simple unit of categorization. One of the few actors playing themselves in the film, Julie Christie, cannot even get credit for being herself, as Connie pierces the "movie star" role she plays: "Come on, Haven, she can't even comb her hair." Invited onstage at The King of the Road nightclub by (the "real") Vassar Clements, she passes in one shot behind a black pole that splits the performance space, as if stepping momentarily into an identity void. "Can you see me?" she asks the audience. "I can't see you." Then she sings her final song, an ode to the non-character type she exemplifies: "Rolling stone, rolling stone gathers no moss. / But neither does it gather any love." Connie is the subjective nothing and nobody prior to the fictional social links that give characters provisional substance, or the illusion of inner life that movies never actually (*can* never) directly show. When you compare a film to a novel, you might despair at how comparatively slight cinema's resources are for representing minds. Connie is yet another symptom of the extra flattening that happens in network films, but we should also recognize the different kind of realism that results. Altman's characters are not like the best friends or intimate lovers we try to persuade ourselves we find on screen, or through text. Connie, despite her celebrity, is *more* common in the sense that her reflective surface without readable depth characterizes most of the people we encounter in our densely networked world. Just because we exercise our theories of mind, a skill we use every day and every time we encounter a fictional character, does not mean we always succeed at finding meaning where we assume it is. As Bordwell puts it, "Our skills in tracking social relationships and surmising what others think are aroused by nearly all narratives, but we get a real workout in [network tales]."[36] Sometimes the weight is too just too much to lift and we have to give up on some people, or just enjoy them speculatively.

Haven is another case in point. He troubles traditional models of character influence. On a simple, static character network graph measured by direct (close or intimate) interaction, his node would look unremarkable, if still relatively central. But we know from his first scene in the studio that he does not go much for two-way communication. He does, however, leave his marker all across town, analogized by the "HH" horseshoe flower arrangement he brings to the airport and has sent to Barbara Jean's hospital room, the biggest one in sight. Hal Phillip Walker, as we have already noted, is a character network of his own without a body, not just a booming PA voice but a series of mentions, stickers, buttons, and supernumerary volunteers. The music industry as much as the political machine, we have already noted, turns person into commodity—relations between people into relations between things, in a Marx paraphrase—and so we should also account for the dissemination of character voice and image throughout the film, via radio, record, and television. And, notably if more locally, through the telephone. In one of several phone conversations in the film—another pronounced telecommunicational link is built between Del, Triplette, and their contacts—Tom begins his attempted seduction of Linnea by placing a couple of ill-timed calls to her house. Like Connie's, Tom's inner life is completely inscrutable, even void. His voice circulates and enters bedrooms, like Connie's does for Barbara Jean, through the radio. In Tom's brief phone conversations with Linnea, the former remains entirely off-screen. Audio engineer Jim Webb developed an ingenious system for these scenes, removing the speaker transmitter from Tomlin's on-camera phone and having Carradine in a separate room listening to her live via earphones through a microphone replaced by the transmitter. Talking back into his phone's transmitter, Tomlin hears him live as well. "It's the perfect system because you can do it in real time and sound isn't leaking into anything."[37] Too much technical information, maybe, but it reveals something important about the way *Nashville*'s character network is pieced together. Down to their visual and sonic inventions that hold the noisy field in vibrating place, Altman and crew carve into every scene channels that link individual characters in tentative relief from their environmental and social surrounds. The combination of momentary clarity and live dialogue through a phone, set in real time against the awkward domestic sounds of a husband and children in an adjacent room (Del eventually listens in, completing an uncomfortable triangle), constructs an asymmetrical, dynamic scene as much as a straightforward, mutual connection between two characters.

Perhaps most importantly, the scenic mobility of nomadic characters like Walker, the Tricycle Man, Opal, L. A. Joan, and Kenny stitch diegetic locations into a mesh and thereby establishes a wider cognitive map of scenes proximate in space or time. A static network graph might reveal the extent of their character links, but it does not add any information we do not already have about how they assist in forming the network in the first place. And the worst thing about a network diagram is that the nodes and links all look mostly the same. They occupy different relational positions in the web, they might take on different sizes, they have larger or smaller degrees of connectivity. Character, however, is not only a proper name. Character is the set or collection of intrinsic qualities of a narrative agent (what Latour would call an actant), who enters at some point, in the path of a narrative's discourse, a network made up of other agents. Those qualities or characteristics influence the way the agent behaves in the network. Cinematography, sound design, and editing not only frame behavior but provide the primary basis for its existence in the diegesis. Character, then, is whatever a network diagram fails to show.

Opal, from the British Broadcasting Company

In one origin story for Geraldine Chaplin's Opal, Altman and Tewkesbury witnessed the actress and first daughter of silent film royalty hounded by paparazzi at Cannes. But instead of playing one of the reporters who swarm film festivals and corner the stars, Chaplin would play something much more ambiguous: a journalist who may not actually have the credentials to be one. In other words, a reporter without the (professional) right to report. Altman saw the character as a version of himself, as Chaplin says: "The original idea was that I was to do an absolute takeoff on Robert Altman in the movie. He said, 'In this movie, you're me. I just want you to follow me around, watch me, and imitate me.'"[38] Opal does not actually serve as the film's interior narrator. She is more like the parodic idea of one. Like the Walker van does at the formal level of the establishing shot, Opal provides a barely motivated reason for a scene, what Altman pragmatically describes as "the reason why 'I' showed up, my camera." She is a meta-presentation of the cinematic impulse to show someone or something without formal reciprocity.

To return to Hamilton's studio recording at the film's outset: Opal's presence disturbs Haven enough—"She's breakin' my concentration"—that he asks his son to usher her out of Studio A and into the smaller, cramped Studio B, where Linnea Reese is recording a raucous gospel tune ("Do You Believe in Jesus? (Yes, I Do)") with the Fisk Jubilee Singers. The structure of the scene at this point crosscuts between A and B—between country and gospel; white and Black religious expression; stolid, humorlessly martial song frozen in a nonexistent past and lively, upbeat, and up-tempo joy that galvanizes the present in choral voice and dance (the last contrast marked by Opal in racist terms so on-the-nose and apparently sincere that it is hard not to laugh at it/her, even while being appalled. But despite her offensively fetishistic comments, there is a certain sense in which she's right. She recognizes, as perhaps a non-American more easily can, how foundational Black music is to American music as such, how central its nodes really are. Opal will play this diagnostic role several more times in the film). Niemi remarks compellingly on the "failure" of Hamilton's recording as a failure of "the hegemonic American narrative" to coalesce, "a failure of Gesellschaft, an authoritarian corporate structure that functions through top-down discipline and money incentives" rather than "any shared vision of community or higher purpose."[39] Studio A and B are like two Americas, coexisting side by side with a soundproofed wall between them.

If Studio A is the country music industry's ideological skin meant to cover over and drown out the spirit chambered away in Studio B, the bewilderingly naïve visitor Opal ties the two together by making Haven (begrudgingly) open the door that separates them. For a reporter, she appears to know little to nothing specific about American music. But it is precisely because she is an empty(headed) vehicle for the cameras and

FIGURE 7 *Studio A.*

microphones to follow that her presence on set links two chambers that would otherwise have remained sealed from one another. Opal's movements are another miniature key for the network capacities of Altman's filmmaking, which here appears to follow and respond to them; a combination of tracking, cutting, and sonic overlap are revealed as networking tools for linking people, locations, and even alternative song traditions and expressive styles that larger, imaginary cultural hegemonies work to structure in the form of hierarchies. A and B are economic as well as sociocultural designations; in the structure of the scene, though, B follows A as a return of its repressed, opening interpretive channels between them, revealing two-way interactions. There would be no A, no two hundred years to sing about, without the existence of B.

Opal, like Connie or the Tricycle Man, is barely an individual. Which doesn't mean she's not a striking figure. She's a comic Dickensian caricature, which ensemble films pressure their characters into becoming, since there is only so much time to get to know them personally beyond their most salient traits, repetitions, tics, and compulsions. Which is why her most memorable appearances are monologues. They are time-

FIGURE 8 *Studio B.*

spaces where Opal can spread her human-interest journalistic wings. In the end, she just reinforces the extent of the spoof. "I'm wandering in a graveyard," she says into her handheld microphone, walking and looking around an uncountable number of smashed car bodies piled up in an auto junkyard. This is the endgame of the American spectacle Opal opined on earlier in the film when the pileup was still a nexus of living bodies. Her doggerel is almost impressively assonantal: "Their vast, vacant skeletons sadly sighing to the sky." The cars, she thinks, are trying to communicate to her, and as she apostrophizes their calls Kenny emerges from inside the pileup, assuming Opal is talking to him. Which embarrasses her, at first, the way someone who thinks they are alone with their self-consciousness feels retroactively invaded by the smothering otherness of a subject who one finds has been there all along. Not to worry, though, since (his violin case would suggest) he is a musician, and so another interview subject. The scene ends not with a conclusion to her monologue but with the two of them walking off-screen mid-sentence, Opal's recorder still running. The film cuts to another site of down-home Americana, the stock car racing track, but Opal's commentary does not cut. Her internal narration is the logic of montage radicalized.

Taking us from the ghost shells of mid-century muscle-car dreams to the roar of souped-up engines, the scene cut follows the logic of Opal's bad, sincere poetry (Chaplin recalls that Altman told her to write her monologues "as if you were really serious. Really try and write poetry . . . then it'll be really crappy"[40]). Opal is our farcical Virgil, the infernal tour guide who tries a little too hard but is still informative enough to get a modest tip at the end from gullible patrons. Her tape recorder, if we could play it back entirely, would provide a record of *Nashville*'s sonic fabric: monologues interrupted, noise invading signals, dialogues overlapping, meaning never straightforwardly accessible but always missing something that would complete it, an irony we need to see to confirm but which is only ever hinted at, never spelled out completely.

Network narratives like *Nashville* tend toward unrestricted narration, which means that we have far more information about the social world (at least as far as the cameras and microphones reach into it) than any one character does. That includes Opal, of course, but in some sense she comes closest to embodying our condition (it is a condition, even an affliction, not a perspective) as an audience. Opal knows far less about the town of Nashville than Haven or Barnett or Lady Pearl does, and certainly less about the political machine than Triplette. Her ignorance matches ours, in fact, even as the extent of her movement, observing and recording corners of the story world without stitching them into a seamless fabric, synecdochically mimics the narratorial omniscience of the film's discourse. Opal does not actually know, and does not appear to ever fully learn, how everyone she meets is connected, and we have to admit that some things are going on behind our backs too. At the same time, we are privileged outsiders with Opal's motor, drifting from scene to scene (each scene she's in, that is, is a different social scene). Every film viewer is a tourist visiting the world of the story they are piecing together as they go. Tourists, ignorant as they are, get to see societies with a narrator's eye and ear, paying for their hopeless cultural distance with a nomadic gift for getting around.

24-Track Recording

We never hear Opal's recordings played back, of course. We have, instead, the noisy soundtrack we have, but only because of an important technical experiment. Altman introduced the Lions Gate 8-Track Sound System in the making of the perpetually underrated *California Split* (1974). Jim Webb designed the system for Altman, capitalizing on his experience running sound design for golf broadcasts. The multi-track recording system allowed Altman and his sound team to cut through the noise while retaining its ambience, channeling voices onto separate tracks so that they could play with the levels and direct the listener's attention subtly throughout the sonic crowd. Achieving audio clarity and atmospheric realism at the same time, followable dialogue that seems to emanate from real spatial loci through a thick, circumambient blanket of chatter and din, was an enormous technical feat. It would be matched and exceeded with *Nashville*.[41]

There is one thing about watching (or sensing) Altman films that I love but I know many people hate, or at least find unnecessarily frustrating: hearing what's going on in a scene takes effort. Not in the way learning to sensitively listen to a sonata takes effort. It is more like trying to hear what your friend is saying in a crowded bar. Rick Altman goes as far as to claim that (Robert) Altman "builds his story around twenty-four independent characters" to model his narrative "on the 24-track recording technology commonly used within the music industry":

> Like so many individual sound tracks, separately collected and routed to a common mixing board, the characters never all appear in the same scene until their common appearance at the concluding Parthenon political rally and concert, where the final mix-down can finally be effected. Altman's metaphor for cinema creation is thus based neither in film direction nor in cinematography, but on the process of mixing sound.[42]

While it is a common claim that *Nashville*'s soundscape was recorded on twenty-four tracks, it is not a true one. Sid Levin reports that they used a sixteen-track for some scenes, especially concert and performance sequences, and often a portable eight-track.[43] But twenty-four is a nice number for making the formal connection between character and audio systems. If sound mixing is Altman's "metaphor for cinema creation," or the metaphor's vehicle, its tenor is character—character *as* track, as a layer of a social mix. For Rick Altman the motivation behind the metaphor is anti-hierarchical, a way of resisting the ranking of sounds inherent to classical Hollywood sound design, where "the highest rank among diegetic sounds is accorded to sounds that contribute to the elaboration of the narrative."[44] By leveling the volume of the tracks on the mix, Altman projects a flat ontology of character and event, which puts the film's viewer in a position of relative autonomy. The focal centers of most of *Nashville*'s scenes branch into smaller pockets, so that even the scene unit becomes a small network within a larger one. Our attention fixes on a path to follow within the scene—perhaps consciously, when we find ourselves more interested in some characters than others, though just as often subliminally—inevitably missing most landmarks on the other paths, at least until we rewind or rewatch. In her foreword to the published version of the screenplay, Tewkesbury urges us to "remember that this was written for a visual medium capable of giving assorted information to our perception on so many levels and in so many layers that we can't systematically record it. With that in mind," she continues, "all you need to do is add yourself as the twenty-fifth character [or the twenty-sixth, on my count] and know that whatever you think about the film is right, even if you think the film is wrong."[45]

I want to rewind once again to the movie's primal scene, and the juxtaposition between the two studio recordings. Scene A emphasizes (while deconstructing) the sonic hierarchy Scene B more comfortably inverts. The former emphasizes Haven's song, the latter the din and dialogue outside the recording booth. In the former, speech interrupts song; in the latter, song is the backdrop for speech. But we are also made aware, in both locations, that what we hear is a function of the limits of our attentional field, and that those limits are not just physiological but political. Altman produces and records cinematic sensoria that reveals the significance of what philosopher Jacques Rancière calls "the distribution of the sensible" (*le partage du sensible*). The distribution of the sensible articulates a relationship between perceptual acts and what is socially perceptible, who or what is implicitly deemed worthy of being seen or heard. It is a system, representable as a network, "of self-evident facts of sense perception that simultaneously discloses the existence of something in common and the delimitations that define the respective parts and positions within it," both a common perceptual field and its internal relationships between included participants and excluded non-participants, the seen and heard and the unseen and unheard.[46] Again, in *Nashville* "that's politics," as Walker would and does indeed say, proving it by the means of his own monologue's distribution.

So although Altman disrupts conventional sonic hierarchies throughout the film, he reveals his methodology most explicitly in the recording studio, where ideology is mixed before it is disseminated. The recording apparatuses are foregrounded, both visually and audibly. We see the sound technicians at their boards, close-ups of Volume Unit meters displaying signal levels as they shift and shimmy. Situated outside the isolation booth in Studio B, we hear ratios and volume change as mixers (inside the studio inside the diegetic world) fiddle with the output. Which sutures us aurally into the scene, puts us *there* with the technicians, while also reminding us of the song's mediation, putting us *here*, outside the booth where the singing really happens. Studios A and B make a sonic chiasmus, an analogical torsion or Möbius band where inside-outside and song-speech turn over into their opposites. All is being packaged for realization on the music market. Mediation is, on the one hand, the result of commodification, best marked by Haven's setup and his reaction to Opal: "Let her buy the record." At the same time, the *distributed* network of sounds inside the studio upsets the controlled production hierarchy, the sound isolated and vacuum sealed for pristine *distribution*. There is hardly a better expression of Rancière's political-aesthetic theory to be found.

Take the scene in the Old Time Picking Parlor, which is crosscut with a parallel scene at Deemen's Den. Altman's most innovative device for distributing a vibe throughout a scene is his use of body microphones, in *Nashville* up to eight recording sound at the same time and in the same room. The center of our auditory attention is not only split several ways, but the planned inevitability of overlapping speech and circumambient noise is not aggressively refocused by single shots, which are conventionally used to help us pick dialogue lines out of the mix and attach them to their source characters. Visually, we cut into the venue and the camera pans across a picture of John F. Kennedy hanging on the wall to the stage, where the four-piece Misty Mountain Boys are performing "Mississippi River." Then a creeping zoom-out slowly takes in the crowd. Reverse cut to an angle viewed from the stage and a series of further cuts that reveal the folks in the Parlor: Wade, Haven and Tommy, Bill and Mary, Lady Pearl and Kenny. Meanwhile, at Deemen's Den, the female duo Smokey Mountain Laurel perform "Troubled Times" as Opal circulates with her camera, approaching Tom at a table of blondes. Star, Sueleen, and a bartender named Trout are there too; eventually Albuquerque enters as well. As the parallel scenes unfold, the visual-auditory system approaches thermodynamic equilibrium, a state of high entropy.

Nashville's sonic networks do not entirely negate precisions in staging, blocking, and shot sequencing. But sound, astride and yet off kilter relative to what is shown, is revealed to be the noise in the cinematic system it always already was, since the addition of soundtracks to film in the first place. Right from the opening scenes—when the audience is given the hard sell for the movie they are about to watch, when Walker's PA without a face leaves its garage, when the recording of Haven's patriotic folk song reveals a man who prefers to shake hands via the intermediary of the commodity—we are forced to track a world in which sound is war, a contest for influence replicated on the meta-level of characters' desire to speak, command a scene, and most of all to just sing. In film, do we primarily trust what we see or hear? What about in popular music? Or in electoral politics? What about, *Nashville* prompts, when all three collide?

In Song

We must never forget that song is one of the forms that ties *Nashville* together. At least superficially. Why do critics (and Altman) have to keep telling us that it's a musical, in the end, so many times? ("Any doubts one may harbor that *Nashville* is a musical should be dispelled with the song-driven Opry sequence"[47]). Because it is not *quite* a musical, at least not in its traditional popular mode. All the singing is diegetically motivated. Granted, there are too many numbers to gloss over this feature as if it were incidental to the film's structure. But all the songs are performed by personas internal to the story world—they are performed qua performed. The film's characters sing, but their songs' lyrical voices are the characters' characters. There are no proper arias, no internal monologues, no duets of the truly lovesick and desperate. Just folks putting on a show, for the nice crowd at the Grand Ole Opry and adoring fans around the country.

Still, Altman calls his film a musical. "*Nashville*'s a musical, really," he tells us in his DVD commentary. Which may be less of a genre description than an acute articulation of a desire underlying the film's structure. Granted, even cinema has aspired to music, like every other art has at one time or another—rhythmically, technologically, narratively, or all at once. In its own way, the ensemble film generates a pressure shared by the operatic or musical narrative, to string the whole show on a clothesline of numbers, combining and dispersing characters (plot-characters and voice-characters alike) along the way. *Nashville* does not demand that we suspend our disbelief about any of the performers transitioning from the fictional world into some inner-musical space, stepping outside the ontological boundaries of the diegetic world to address us directly in song ("why are they singing?" every child asks at least once). Still, it uses some of the formal conventions of popular (American) musicals to map its network as it unfolds toward its grand finale.

Pauline Kael's advance review of the film claimed that "not only do [the actors] do their own singing but most of them wrote their own songs—and wrote them in character."[48] This is a legend that kept growing among critics, a bubble of DIY enthusiasm partially popped by Gayle Magee's study of Altman's soundtracks.[49] It is too simple to say, as Altman does in the liner notes to the twenty-fifth anniversary release of the soundtrack on CD, that "each performer wrote their songs from the character's point of view." Several song lyrics, including some of the most memorable tunes, were composed before the making of the film, for instance. But many of Altman's actors did write or participate in the writing of songs they or other cast members would perform; in spirit, if not in every case, the film showcases an improvisatory tendency and open experimental field for characters to find themselves through musical performance.

The mythic aspect of *Nashville*'s collaborative musical ethos may be less of an exaggeration than an apt expression of the film's ironic folk spirit, flowing through its networked veins like good dope. Of the three main subgenres articulated in Rick Altman's magisterial study of the American film musical—the fairy tale musical, the show musical, and the folk musical—*Nashville* is characterized as a meta-modern version of the last because of its social realism, its familial and communal focus, and its creation of an "intermediary space [between American history and pure dream, fantasy, or utopia] which we designate by such terms as tradition, folklore, and Americana."[50] It should be obvious that, just as the ontological status of song and number in *Nashville* differentiates it from musical proper, where "too much realism threatens a film's identity as a musical," its tonal disposition keeps unfeigned folk musical Americana (*Summer Stock, Summer Holiday, Meet Me in St. Louis, Oklahoma!*) at an arm and a half's length.

In the traditional musical, speech is the vehicle for action and plot development while song is narratively static. In song, nothing much happens except passionate utterance, self-reflection, the expression of a personal trait or motivation, and the inhabitation of a state of mind or mood. Song occupies the furthest pole of self-consciousness. In conventional opera, the aria stops time (even *internalizes* time) and takes us into minds or souls revealing themselves, while recitative drives the plot forward. The traditional aria expands the musical repertoire, complexifying basic melodies or motifs into sections, movements, turns, variations, recapitulations, and cabalettas. But no singer in Nashville nakedly bears the beating of their character's mind, let alone their soul (until, maybe, *maybe* the very end of the film). I am not criticizing the songs themselves, though many have.[51] It is irrelevant to judge the music by the generic standards of polished, spit-shined country. What we have instead is the mess in the process, the improvisations and failures behind the mass-marketable tentpole products, the unvarnished collective life behind the shining stars. The songs are not all good, though some are clearly worse than others, and that's just the point. Though saying so won't satisfy the keepers of Nashville sincerity.

One of the most dramatic, pathos-filled song sequences in the film involves two intercut scenes, one at Exit/In and the other at the Chaffin's Barn Dinner Theater. Tom Frank, who performs at the Exit/In first with his trio and then without, is both link and rupture, a roving two-beat force of connection and disconnection. The one-night stand is his existential (anti-) form. He embodies, without betraying any inner life, the difference between the superficial and the subliminal, revealed first in his call to Linnea's house, made while his hook-up Opal is still in the room. Tom also offers a theory of song as weak social glue, as the lyric correlative of his role in *Nashville*'s character system. He is not *of* the Nashville culture in the first place, and Tewkesbury's initial script even began with Tom in midtown Manhattan meeting record company execs before heading South to capitalize on the country-western explosion. His "It Don't Worry Me"—written by Carradine himself, first performed on the set of *Thieves Like Us*, and a seed of inspiration for Altman to take on a music project in the first place—plays over the radio throughout the film. It is a hobo drifter's (or maybe just a slacker's) chorale for the dream of aimless social atomism. A casual, wish-fulfilled dismissal of collective pain in the blues-folk tradition. Perhaps it is also a counter-populist entry into Walker's write-in contest for a new national anthem: "The price of bread may worry some / But it don't worry me / Tax relief may never come / But it don't worry me // Economy's depressed, not me / My spirit's high as it can be / And you may say that I ain't free / But it don't worry me." The audience at the club chants its refrain when Tom is welcomed up on stage to play a few.

Which is awkward because Bill and Mary didn't know he was there. He's been avoiding them, trying to do his own thing. But when you're pulled out of a crowd, onto a stage as the solo act, you're more visible than ever. Relations come out of hiding too. Opal lets Mary know that she's slept with Tom (or, as she puts it, they "got to know each other in the Biblical sense"). Tom calls Bill and Mary up to play a tune, "Since You've Gone," which says everything one needs to know about all the hurt festering between the three of them, speaking the truth none of them can say out loud, at least not without first donning the mask of song. It is apparent too in Mary's ice-cold face, in the way she clears her throat, and in the way the camera breaks the trio by cutting from a longer shot to medium shots of Tom and Mary and Mary and Bill. The fractured triangle, which here is seen rather than heard, models mediated desire, its circuit through promiscuous networks, never achieving its aims except by indirection. Mary turns to Tom, away from Bill, as if to make the song's lyrics transparently communicative rather than performative: "Since you've gone, my heart is broken another time." If Bill, looking down at his guitar, is willfully oblivious, Tom refuses to meet her gaze, looking past her the whole time, unfazed. And if we sympathize with Mary most, the camera cuts to Tom's current love project, Linnea, sitting in the back of the club with Wade, and then his previous one, Opal. The audiovisual surround always turns intimacy back into promiscuity.

Then we cut to the "smoker," the male-dominated Walker fundraiser where Sueleen is lowered onto the stage from the ceiling and expected, unbeknownst to her, to perform a striptease. What unfolds here is worse than the scene at the Exit/In. In a span of minutes Sueleen experiences the collapse and tenuous restoration of her self-image as a female performer and rising star. Rick Altman calls it, appropriately, a "psychological striptease."[52] Her painful rendition of "I Never Get Enough" crosscuts with and against Tom's next song, "I'm Easy." Tom's lyrics are desires of the other, not his own (whereas Mary's performance spoke the literal truth of her feelings toward Tom in the guise of performance)—the broken trio models and sets in motion a sequence of mediated desire clinched by the camera's own wandering eye. What's more, the formal dynamics of the parallel scenes rub against the other in disharmonious frottage. Tom dedicates his number to an unnamed person in the audience, sending the camera off to glance at all the female candidates for the honor. Mary, Opal, and L. A. Joan each briefly take the message on their own behalves. But then, failing to triangulate Tom's look, their own, and the camera's, each turns around to search for his true target. Tom is performing his power as a hub in the film's character network.

The camera, we must conclude, does not quite line up with Tom's performative look; instead, it catches each lover in a relay of mimetic desire, formalizing male desire as perpetually seeking another object and female desire or rivalry as the gas for its engine. His eyeline is not properly matched for us, but as the three women closer to the stage look around and back we are led to believe (as they are) that he's looking at Linnea, always framed off-center through an out-of-focus foreground of faces. Linnea need not question that she is caught by Tom's look (finally lining up with the camera's view), seated in the back of the club, framed only by the rear wall. Cutting back to Tom, we see how he looks obliquely off-screen to his right while Linnea looks back through the center of the frame from the left. How do we piece this spatial field together? By recognizing, I think, that the scene is composed to generate an awareness on our part that the formation of character relationships is adulterated (and *adultered*) by provisionality. In this world and in this film, people connect, use each other, and start over again without achieving a sense of completion, satisfaction, or peace. Networks alienate as much as they harmonize. Linnea, temporarily, for at least one scene, occupies the special, formal position of the leading lady, or at least the leading dude's romantic counterpart. We know, because the visual form teaches us, that nobody is special forever. As Helene Keyssar puts it, this is a "story only moving pictures could tell," where "the moving camera captures the transformation" in each woman's illusion and subsequent disillusion.[53]

At the smoker the setup is inverted, as if the two scenes are projected onto each other through a convex mirror. If Tom's performance gives him control over his female audience, the howling male audience at the smoker frames the infernal fantasy Sueleen descends into. The camera circles Sueleen, as if occupying various points in the surrounding vantage of men leering, whistling, and demanding that she take it all off. If, at the Exit/In, the camera slowly approaches the male point of view by circulating through the network of desired female objects, each entertained and then discarded, here the camera begins by mimicking the male audience's participatory ogling only to turn itself back onto the crowd (in ambivalent disgust?) when the female disillusionment becomes too painful, too bare and naked. The camera keeps its distance when Delbert whispers her a promise to open for Barbara Jean, and again when she, after accepting with teary resignation, takes off her underwear. If we got what *we* wanted, even just to laugh at the vulnerably unaware rube, we feel the sting of its ethical price. Sueleen temporarily escapes from the room, but we know the room will follow her down further. And we stay behind, with the hoots and hollers, with a sense of helpless passivity, no more admirable than anyone else in the scene. As Keyssar recognizes, a traditional sequential edit between the Exit/In and the Dinner Theater would have adequately communicated a simple truth about the prevalence of male sexual objectification and the pressures, both internal and external, that lead women to acquiesce to it (and desire it in turn). The painful success of the joint scene, however, depends on our capacity to expand our attentional field, to compare alternative means by which cinematic information is routed, and thereby "to care about more than one person at a time, to care deeply, and to care differently."[54] If we cannot care infinitely, hands across *Nashville*, at least we can seek the furthest limits of our moral concern.

Network film, by virtue of its sideways-shuffling narrational form, affords a distributional pathos or "care" (I have preferred to call it attention) that traditional protagonist-driven films seal off. Sueleen and Tom's cross-cut performances, edited so that we occupy the epistemic position not of an audience member

FIGURE 9 *Linnea looks back.*

at either locale but of someone peeking through apertures into both in turn, reveal a deeper logic governing song repertoire as a discursive vehicle for narrative networking. At several points in *Nashville*, two or more opposed psychological positions—glimpsed only briefly through the mediation of semi-fictive lyric expression—are juxtaposed sequentially, often across the boundary of sex or gender difference, a point already noted by Richard Ness:

> In many cases songs sung by the women can be seen as responses to those of the male characters. The independence and optimism expressed in "Bluebird" and "Keep A-Goin'" are answered by the helplessness and despair of "Memphis" and "Dues," while the consequences described in "Rolling Stone" are the result of the cavalier attitude expressed in "I'm Easy." Barbara Jean's final number "My Idaho Home" seemingly ventures into Haven's territory in its emphasis on a traditional family environment, though it contrasts with the hypocritical patriarchal position of "For the Sake of the Children" and in its final lyrics reinforces matriarchal control.[55]

If Ness is right about Barbara Jean's final song, about how it interacts as a micro-node in the web of all the film's numbers,

FIGURE 10 *Sueleen at the smoker.*

then we might have discovered a cynical and depressing reason why she ends up serving as *Nashville*'s sacrificial victim.

This Section Brought to You By: Goo Goo Clusters!

The original Goo Goo Cluster, Nashville's official candy and the Grand Ole Opry's official sponsor for Haven Hamilton's show with Tommy Brown and Connie White, is a delicious amalgamation of milk chocolate, caramel, peanuts, and marshmallow nougat. It is a small world in candy form. It succeeds as an assemblage because the cluster's parts are in cahoots with one another while maintaining their distinctness. The Goo Goo Cluster is a sweet, toothsome model for the heterogeneous unities that make up *Nashville*'s character network.

What I'm really saying is that the Goo Goo Cluster is a candy in the form of a musical band, a mini ensemble. There is a rhythm section (caramel and peanuts), a flashy soloist (marshmallow), and a bandleader that holds it all together (milk chocolate). If that sounds like the kind of thing one would see in an old movie palace ad animation, it is also an Altman-style throwaway gag. If we take it seriously for a minute, we might glimpse a sticky truth about the magic of a good musical group, held together by little more than confectionary glue. How to strike that fragile balance between identity and difference without tipping too far in either direction, toward either bland uniformity or chaotic multiplicity?

We have already seen the question asked of the broken trio, a folk group-cum-love triangle. Looking at the music scene writ large, we might conclude that there's a fundamental structural asymmetry that keeps *Nashville*'s network humming. The Goo Goo Cluster is the commodified ideal, not the reality that melts in your hands. In the centerpiece Opry scene, shot and mic'd in the form and style of a concert documentary, three singers perform—Tommy, Haven, and Connie (who replaces the bedridden Barbara Jean)—and as they rotate their sets, their respective entourages on the long stage benches rotate with them. This is Opry tradition, or at least a simulacrum of it, but it is also uncannily suggestive of political theater. The Grand Ole Opry is a big tent, to be sure. But there is no stable center, no unifying moral message, as much as Haven plays the part of ringleader and Nashville/*Nashville*'s stern but fair father ("For the sake of the children," he sings, he must bid his mistress goodbye).

If anything, the Opry songs are joined together by the emcees' live radio advertisements, by nothing less than the Goo Goo Cluster itself. Its light-up sign atop the stage serves as the audience applause sign between acts; the Goo Goo jingle covers over stage transitions between the performers. Altman's manner of shooting and recording people *as clusters* rather than through traditional close-up reverse cutting is chaotic and ragged, often to the point of untidiness. Because the movie's audiovisual field resists simplification and clarification, new binding agents are required to manage the chaos. It is not just that Hollywood film loves singularizing close-ups; America loves them. Celebrity culture demands them, artificial as we nevertheless know them to be. They are the vein into which we inject our most fragile fantasies. In order that those fantasies take on the minimal amount of reality they need to avoid falling apart, something from outside our inner-screen projection must come in and stitch otherwise meaningless ideological fragments together into staged sequence. Into, that is, the appearance of narrative. The Goo Goo Cluster is a dumb, delicious little spot of sugary abjection that binds the audience to the spectacle, turning sentimental lyrics and preening performativity into the story of American unity.

The scene at the Opry is a tour de force of applied concert documentary form, with all the conventional stage angles giving it the appearance of reality pierced by high artifice. Unlike in actual concert docs, we see boundaries form between the small cluster of billed performers (expanded, perhaps, to include their entourages) and the excluded, envious would-be players always there in the wings, in the crowd, somewhere in a dingy bar, or laid up and inactive. Including cuts to locations like Barbara Jean's hospital room, Altman literalizes the dynamic that inevitably emerges in network films, where too many people compete for scarce screen time. That scarcity of discourse time, in turn, formalizes extra-textual, social struggles for recognition in a world where a sense of statistical panic, of individuality lost in seas upon seas of human data, exacerbates the anxieties attendant on more basic drives for self-preservation and -actualization. It is no psychoanalytic secret that we often imagine ourselves to be the world's leading men and ladies; network films knock *every* star off their high horses and give them the supporting roles we're all forced to play. Which is not to say that our social universe is democratic; it just lacks true protagonists. Weak node resentment goes from simmer to boil in Barbara Jean and Barnett's ugly hospital ward argument. Provoked by Connie's pinch-hit performance coming through on the radio, Barbara Jean starts hurling bouquets at her manager-husband, "goin' nutsy" on him, rupturing and then tentatively reestablishing through ritualized forgiveness the delicate, volatile balance they have surely tuned over hundreds of near-breakdowns. It is one of a few relationships in the film where the seat of power is totally ambiguous (Tom and Linnea, I would hazard, is another).

In *Nashville*, we might now say, ideology structures less what people say or think than how they form clusters, the small and only temporary social worlds designed to insulate insiders from outsiders. Not just as a preference, either, but of necessity: if there are not enough young, wealthy, attractive men with property in the world of an Austen novel, in *Nashville* there just aren't enough recording contracts and there isn't enough space in the studio or on the Opry stage for everyone. And if that sounds like a music industry problem only, what do you think happens when movies expand to take a cross-section of that industry's meshwork? The more comprehensive your canvas, the more crowded your shots and soundscapes become.

FIGURE 11 *The Grand Ole Opry, brought to you by Goo Goo.*

Altman groups his characters around tables so often to give his story world some order—the efficient if interminable order of conversation—but as anyone who has braved a public-school cafeteria knows, there is only so much room at the table too. And just because you have a seat now does not mean you are guaranteed one tomorrow, or at the next show. We might call these small world dynamics the film's musical group form. Sadly, even good bands break up once they have gone as far with each other as they possibly can. And Goo Goo Clusters are delicious, but you've gotta eat 'em fast or else they'll melt.

The Women of *Nashville*

It was Joan Tewkesbury's sense that the world of *Nashville* orbits around its women. In her interview with Stuart, she describes Albuquerque, L. A. Joan, Mary, and Opal as "facets of the same diamond," all "girls looking to get out of these hideous little lives that were just coming out of the fifties."[56] They are facets of the same second-wave feminist example, struggling to break into post-domesticity around the time the

Equal Credit Opportunity Act hatched in Congress. Which is not to say the women of *Nashville* are in simple solidarity with one another. Looking at one facet of a diamond means the rest are hidden from view, or only peripherally visible, even as they also make up a hidden unity.

By name, Lady Pearl is the whole precious feminine object unto herself. She dresses like she's doing her own thing, in royal purples and red-pinks, like someone turned the dial on all the bicentennial bunting décor and found her on another channel. Really, if there is anyone in the film whose mind is truly elsewhere it's Pearl. Her proximity to Haven and her proprietorship of the Picking Parlor places her at the center of *Nashville*'s character network. Still, she often seems in but not *of* this world. She stands in the way of Haven taking political sides—at least until Triplette finally offers him a chance at the biggest job in Nashville, the governorship—all while nursing a glassy-eyed torch for the "Kennedy boys" and their Camelot ("But they were different . . ."). At times Pearl seems as much out of time as the Kennedys, maintaining connections with the Chamber of Commerce, the high school twirlers, and all the local country acts but sidelined by Haven whenever he has bigger fish to fry, like with Delbert and Triplette. She attends Catholic mass, spending Sunday away from the boys. When they are together, the more she talks the more Haven wishes she would shut up. That's the rough pattern for all the women in tense partnerships with men, though Barbara Jean and Barnett's overlapping personal and business relationship erupts and cools while Pearl and Haven coexist at a simmer, keeping their distance (after getting out of their Jeep, at least) within the several scenes they share.

Most of the men in the film are either dealmakers or drifters. Not everyone is so easy to put into one category or another (Bud? Tommy?), but you can—Bud is a drifter at heart with dreams that don't fit the life his daddy has plotted out for him, and one feels, if we were to catch up with the still-living characters a decade later, he would finally be pursuing a singing career wherever it took him; Tommy is a man who has kept his true thoughts to himself and his community in order to play nice with the white establishment. A network graph would show both types as heavily connected characters (as everyone in the ensemble is, in *Nashville*, at least quantitatively), but the dealmaker type is connected the way members of several corporate boards of directors are, while the drifters are like the people who know everyone in the neighborhood because they're out on the street, walking around all day. The primary female dichotomy—which, like with the men, is more of a spectrum with two poles than a distinction with a secure border—is between those who have control over the kind and amount of attention they get and those who do not.

One theory of the film's exceptional scenes—the ones, I mean, that are powerful for being intimate, pathos-weighted exceptions rather than part of *Nashville*'s noisy, chaotic main thruway—is that they pack emotional punch by isolating two characters from the wider network (often one man and one woman, though never in a wholesome heterosexual couple way) whose power claims on each other are ambiguous. Who really is using whom between Tom and Linnea? Who really holds the strings, Barnett-as-daddy or Barbara Jean-as-fragile-child? Who is more doomed, Wade the angry realist or Sueleen the naïve fantasist? The truths of the matter are in the uncertainties, not in clear, axiomatic answers. There are public faces and private ones; which are more real? Network films tend to offer something different on the question of gender than traditional character analysis usually knows how to find. What Tewkesbury called her female characters' "hideous little lives" are not given whole in *Nashville*; we do not have tragic backstories or even full enough identities to interpret without imagining their life histories creatively from the smallest fragments of their present days. If we think of characters in the network as personality molecules with untold histories, forming and re-forming compounds with all the other little motes, we lose the aspect of gender that involves a psychologically complex, personal negotiation of an individual's self-image in tension with another individual's imagined image (the stuff of romance and melodrama). But we gain insights into social concepts like gender at a different scale, as pattern rather than precious inner truth.

Extras and Supernumeraries

In the firmament of a film built from a broad constellation of stars, dimmer bulbs insist that we reflect on their function in the character network too. Altman, for one, had a ragtag way of casting extras and bit players. An uncountable number of local musicians, medical professionals, proprietors and small businesspeople, security guards, Shriners, and drifters would make their way on screen. Sometimes they played versions of themselves. But Alan Rudolph created miniature scenarios for each super-numerical actor to follow, in detail disproportionate to their screentime, which would often take up just a flicker of a moment. These characterizations were, to paraphrase George Eliot, roars on the other side of silence. Their conversational lines, whether picked up by sound mics or not, were improvised but motivated by Rudolph's scenarios. In this way they were microscopic versions of the film's main characters. Harry Haun, researching the making of *Nashville* for a *Los Angeles Times* article, was tapped to be a part of the Dinner Theater crowd during Sueleen's rendition of "Let Me Be the One":

> Ushering him into a seat down front, Rudolph briefed him. "Okay, now, you're a field man working for ABC/Paramount. Your boss is down in Nashville from New York and you want to impress him by taking him and his wife to this little dive on lower Broadway. And you're telling him all about this great singer he's going to hear . . ." Haun sat down next to the fictional boss and the missus, getting into character. As Gwen Welles ascended the stage and proceeded to croak wretchedly through her song, Haun realized that

his position at ABC/Paramount was on the line. His entire body crumpled in dismay. "If you look closely," says Haun with discernible pride, "you can see my elbow go limp in silhouette."[57]

This is fun stuff. It's also a window into the way extras function in the film—less as background reality-effect than as untapped potential links in an entropic story world. The network is potentially endless, as Henry James said about reality outside of fiction. *Nashville*'s supernumeraries reveal that fact without insisting on it to the detriment of the viewer's capacity to track the difference between foreground and background inherent to any narrative.

In *Nashville*, there is a porous membrane between the extras and the ensemble, occasionally traversed in the span of single scenes. One theory of the minor character (on the spectrum from brief scripted role to extra) is essentially a labor theory: a character's relative disappearance into the background of the story world is structurally analogous to a worker's disappearance into their functional role in a labor process. The "labor," in this formula, is story labor, regardless of whether the character is working, whether their role is to be a worker in the traditional sense. Some historians of the novel have pointed out that servants (like messengers in ancient and early modern dramas) fulfill a particular function in novel discourse, often going unnamed but providing essential services: lubricating the plot's path by arranging for scenes to take place, connecting principal characters, arranging essential encounters.[58] Class, rank, or status is an obvious way character networks can be sorted into center and periphery, though this changes historically as the kinds of stories people tell, and the types of characters that come into and out of focus, shifts. In *Nashville*, Opal, the one British character, offers a class-based explanation for how the social network gets sorted. At the Exit/In, seated next to Opal, chauffeur Norman tries to flaunt his access to the town's real inner life, offering to take her around: "I could tell you things that would send you around the corner." "Please, Norman," Opal begs, "I make it a point never to gossip with servants."

Opal, as always, hyperbolizes the truth. Network form works by flattening traditional status hierarchies, substituting a gradation of character influence based on the accumulation of links. Nobody in *Nashville* is truly insulated from anybody else; there is just a scarcity of time for certain characters to traverse the degrees of separation between themselves and their favorite stars and power players. There is still a residual trace of the good ol' Southern-agrarian class system, visible in scenes like Haven's estate barbecue, which is crashed by working-class Albuquerque looking for a hot meal (reading as "white trash" to the well-dressed folks, just like she will when she tries to get backstage at the Opry) and serviced by a tokenized Wade in dinner jacket and bow tie. But despite Haven's best efforts, that world is in the descendant, attested by the unwelcome presence of "unexpected guest(s)" like Albuquerque, Tricycle Man, and a gauchely gregarious Opal begging guest star Elliot Gould (who appears to have walked out of another Altman film and into this one) for an interview. Her observation that the surroundings evoke the death-ridden country mansion in Bergman's *Cries and Whispers* surely clinches the verdict.

Supernumeraries make up the crowds that ensemble characters labor to differentiate themselves from (at the airport, at the Opry, at the smoker, at the Parthenon). But they may also exist in the film as (nearly-)silent singularities who mediate character interactions. Linnea's children are exemplars, telling stories, primarily via sign language, from their day at school while also conveying by their presence the fragility of the middle-class family unit. Linnea clearly loves them dearly, but Delbert is a bit uncomfortable (if well-meaning) in his fatherly habitat, awkward with his daughter, short with his son, and alienated from both through his lack of American Sign Language (ASL) fluency. As the boy tells how he passed his swimming test and his sister sets the table for dinner, Triplette is in the other room booking Sueleen to "entertain the troops" at the fundraiser. In a moment, Linnea will go the same phone to receive Tom's initial pick-up call, the first step in her subsequent affair. The almost too-sentimental function of the children is to cast four other characters' centrifugal attentions in motion, revealing—as if with invisible ink—the unspoken emotional drift at the center of hearth and home. Nuclear families, celebrated as America's bedrock unit in songs by Haven and Barbara Jean, are flimsy shelters against external pressures—casual sex, excessive work, unchristian pop imagery.

But most of the film's minor characters, cameos by Gould and Christie aside, do not occupy the social center of the scenes they appear in. They are either one of the many, disappearing into a hungry mass representative of the American public writ large (dwarfing, as a totality, the ensemble characters sprinkled in among them), or singular mediating functions, usually with somewhere between zero and two lines. This is how things work in most narratives, with the exception that here—and this is thematic to the larger view of network narratives I have been advancing—the mediation appears in and of itself. Witness the unnamed nurse kicking Kelly out of Barbara Jean's hospital room with nothing more than an acrid glance, as if doing the bidding not just of the ward she works in but of the protocols of the character network as such. Above all these extra-ensemble actors serve to arbitrate implicit relational claims to influential characters; witness too the Opry security guard who holds Albuquerque back from getting too close to Connie before the latter takes the stage. Supernumeraries separate the stars from the fans and the wannabes. They are the official agents of the network's infrastructure, policing the directionality of certain charged links (to advance the metaphor, they are like cops on traffic duty). Sometimes, like mini-Triplettes or Lady Pearls, they hold the keys to the peripheral stages around town. There is the aforementioned barkeep Trout, who greases Sueleen's slide into humiliation at the smoker, and given his particular sense of humor we can reasonably imagine that he had his hand in getting Albuquerque a chance to sing unheard, drowned out by the noise of the motor speedway.

How many middlemen disappear into the absent background of any narrative discourse? Film is already democratic, compared to written stories, because at least we get to see in it the extras, the workers, the functional members of every story world that, in a necessarily unequal system with scarce attentional resources, go unnamed. Network cinema, which gives our social networking muscles an extra workout, directs more of our attention toward those essential staffers who hide in plain sight, but without whom the entire world would collapse. Politics and popular music are two domains, sold as a star system, where the presence-in-absence of background operatives emerge as both form and theme.

What's in the Violin Case?

Internet message board theories aside, we never learn what's in the mysterious *Pulp Fiction* briefcase. Violin cases are much easier, at least for anyone who's seen a few 1930s Warners gangster flicks or Disney's post-Prohibition Mickey's Amateurs short with Donald Duck. It's a gun, stupid. Probably of the Thompson variety.

In *Nashville*, Kenny's ubiquitous violin case is not just a character prop. It is not only an answerable plot question either. It's a *thing*, taking up a disproportionate amount of the film's discourse space, more than any of the real played or playable musical instruments we see and hear across its city-and-soundscape. Kenny is enough of a loner/sucker/aimless loser type that it really is likely that he's carrying around a violin, maybe an old one, from when he played in a Midwest community children's orchestra his mother encouraged him to join. Maybe his mother compared him a few times too often to Linda's son down the street who earned first chair (*such a nice, polite boy, and so handsome*). If anyone is packing a gun in this film, it is likely to be the other mysterious young man in Mr. Green's orbit, the Barbara Jean-obsessed soldier Glenn, whose last name is easy to mix up with Kenny's first. Both guys have very present absent mothers. Both are what today's teens would call "creepers." Glenn Kelly has already been called a killer, by Tom at the airport ("Kill anybody this week?"). And he cuts a Hinckley-before-Hinckley, unassuming psychopath figure that has only gained in visibility since the mid-1970s. Or is just a brutally common Vietnam-era Post-Traumatic Stress Disorder (PTSD) case, sublimated into twisted love.

There is a moment, perhaps more ominous in retrospect or on third viewing, when Walker's van pulls into its garage for the night, still broadcasting its monologue about the importance of taxing churches and their "vast holdings of land." Kenny walks by Walker HQ, looks up at the campaign banners. The PA voice becomes more spectral as its source disappears behind the garage door. "It will not be easy. But we will bask in the satisfaction of having done what we should have done. And if we don't get it done today, we may run out of tomorrows." Kenny shuffles his violin case in his hands; we cut to a close-up of the object and his caricature portrait on its outer surface; Kenny walks with it off frame.

The cut to the violin case, which is also a close-up of Kenny's drawn avatar, offers a metonymic relationship atypical for Altman. He is his violin case, the shot seems to

FIGURE 12 *Kenny and his violin case.*

say, or he is who he is as a character in proximity to it. It's not the first time we see this image; we can glimpse it at an oblique angle during the traffic jam scene, lying in the backseat of Kenny's car on top of Walker campaign flyers and signs. In a different sort of network film, one with more of a ring topology than the dense mesh of *Nashville*—*Winchester '73* (1950) or *The Red Violin* (1998) come immediately to mind— the case and whatever it contained would circulate through the entire character ensemble. But here, the violin case is a special object because it does not receive that kind of focal emphasis. Whatever sits inside it remains hidden for almost the entire film, locked away just like Kenny's desires, motivations, and goals as a character. Kenny hugs it close, wary of anyone handling it, as if countering the forces of circulation that drive the film discourse he is uncomfortably ensconced in.

Network narratives are particularly knowledgeable about relations—who knows whom, who shares mutual friends, who is on a social collision course—and relatively obtuse about direct motivations. Music, since at least the Romantic era, has often been recruited as the vehicle through which obscure feelings are directly expressed, and heard as the irrepressible outflowing of inner life into a language beyond (or beneath) language. Musicals and film scores often follow opera in flirting with song and melody as hidden emotional truth underlying masquerade, reticence, and social ritual. Until the very end of the film, at least, *Nashville* flaunts how easily music manipulates and how wary one should be about it. Which makes the violin case and its hidden cargo especially curious. In a town where everyone with a modicum of talent is trying to get on stage, Kenny never takes his fiddle out, not even to tune it up. Whatever's inside the case is the objectification of absence amidst all the noise, banter, wailing—amidst, that is, all the marketable expression, everything visible and hearable about the American hustle. It is the inarticulable threat, we might say, that everyone disavows, knowing full well that they've got something coming to them but laughing it off into the future all the same.

In a movie with a narrational range that thrives on the surface of things, where small social worlds are mapped broadly but not deeply—horizontally or side to side, but not vertically—personal talismans are, well, as sketchy as a caricature drawing. The outer shell of Kenny's violin case marks the limitations of network cinema's so-called omniscience. By the time it's unlocked, it's already too late.

Greek Finale

Who is *Nashville*'s goddess Athena? Its *parthénos*, its virgin maiden? Is there only one, or are there many? The film's final scene, its tragic finale, is set at the Parthenon in Nashville's Centennial Park, a full-scale replica of the Greek original, designed by architect and former Confederate sergeant William Crawford Smith and built in 1897 as the city's centerpiece for the Tennessee Centennial and International Exposition. It heralded Nashville as the "Athens of the South," the region's seat of arts and learning. By the country's bicentennial, the Nashville Parthenon gave off more of a postmodern air, of classical pastiche in the land of hot chicken. Its gods, goddesses, heroes, priestesses, and cult objects are pop culture icons—rhinestone cowboys, TV detectives, oracles who riddle in country song.

One might read the film's last scene as a glib switcheroo. The bullet headed, all film long, for Hal Phillip Walker accidentally clips the one person everybody in town cares for. Or claims to, tries to, pretends to, means to. Barbara Jean, the beloved, earnest, unpretentious fan favorite, is cut down instead of the mountebank politician. Accidentally on purpose. *Nashville* has no protagonist, and maybe neither does Nashville, though we have seen that one of the main pressures on the potential symmetries of any character network is the sociopolitical drive toward protagonism, or what we might simply call power and influence. Some characters want to be nodes, and the simplest expression of that in the film is Walker's campaign, which is also appropriately faceless and populist, articulated as the will of the law degree-less people. Does Barbara Jean need to be dispatched, then, because she's special in some way? In a way that's inconvenient for some powerful interest in the world of the story? Or in a way that's inconvenient for the character system that comprises the film's discourse? Ronee Blakley may have been nominated for a Best Supporting Actress Academy Award, but there is something about the character she plays that distinguishes her in the network.

There is a lot of naivete in *Nashville*, but a lot less sincerity. A lot of charisma without the expressive validity to match. Fragile and tenuous though her hold on her public persona may be, Barbara Jean is one of the exceptions. That alone is not why she's tragically shot, why she unbearably becomes this story's Antigone or Cordelia, but it is part of the story. Rewind to an otherwise unspectacular sequence of cuts between four scenes in the middle of the film. First, as Barbara Jean is released via wheelchair from the hospital, Barnett asks (in an upbeat voice that masks the ominous irony) an orderly to take her "cortège" of flowers down the back elevator. We cut to an over-the-shoulder shot of Mr. Green, who has moved through the previous shot's foreground off camera and is now addressed by a nurse, who informs him (to his surprise) that his wife died that morning. His face falls into a look of what seems to me like angry grief. As he processes, Kelly comes over and tells him the good news:

> Mr. Green? Mr. Green, my momma saved her life. They used to live next door to each other . . . my momma's the one that put out the flames. She always loved Barbara Jean more than anything . . . she's still keepin' a scrapbook on her. The only thing she said to me when she joined up, she said, "Son when you're doing your travels, I want you to see Barbara Jean. You don't have to say nothin' about me or nothin' like that, I just want you to see Barbara Jean." So that's what I

been doing. Now I'm gonna go over to Opryland and hear her sing. You give my best to your wife now.

Kelly heads toward the elevator, Mr. Green beings to sob, and we cut quickly to Triplette and Opal inside the Dinner Theater.

In a film like *Nashville*, where so much occurs in deep field and so much is draped in cynicism, you are meant to notice the relatively few moments that unfold up close, where affect is registered on the face rather than subliminally. We glimpse what we take to be real emotion, even if in passing, in Linnea, Mary, Barbara Jean, Barnett, Albuquerque, Lady Pearl, Pvt. Kelly, and Mr. Green. I said earlier that Mr. Green's tragedy as a character is getting sucked into the film's network in the first place. Before the cut, the camera having crept into a close double, Mr. Green is briefly isolated on the right of the frame when the oblivious, well-meaning Kelly walks away. The cut to Triplette and Opal is also a cut from Green's sobs to their laughter, as if to underline a rift between Green and the rest of the world he cannot help having to endure, continuously reminded of the irrelevance of his feelings to a younger generation with cultural tastes he cannot imagine ever pursuing. The film is often edited to reinforce the irony funhouse its characters are trapped in (the church montage is immediately preceded, for instance, by Tom and Mary in bed together, as if the film's discourse is trying to cleanse its story's rotten soul).

But back to the Dinner Theater, and the cut's subliminal signal—emotional authenticity is always covered up by theater, and fast, like water backfilling a crease made by canoe paddle. Mr. Green will feel his feelings, to be sure, but not for us; the further one retreats into pathos, the less one's being is registered by the network. Now, Opal turns off her recording machine; what she's about to say will not be on the record (though of course we hear it, so it certainly *is* on the record too). Don't laugh, *but*: "I have a theory about political assassination. You see, I believe that people like Madame Pearl and . . . all these people here in this country who carry guns are . . . the *real* assassins. Because, you see, they stimulate other people who are perhaps innocent and who eventually are the ones who pull the trigger." Quick cut to the Green house before Triplette is able to respond. Kenny, standing on the threshold between his room and the hallway, is on the phone with his mother. L. A. Joan approaches Kenny in her underwear, crosses over into his room, and circles around him seductively (or at least questioningly, "like a skinny cat" as Tewkesbury's directions say) as we hear his mother on the other end asking where he is. Both women mirror each other, each asking Kenny who he's talking to. Now the interior architecture of the shot matches his situation, caught between two women playing traditional narrative roles—one the superegoic, controlling nag and the other a seductive replacement figure for what we might imagine to be typical hetero-masculine desire. Joan sits on the bed, waiting for him to get off the phone with his mother, while the latter interrogates Kenny, getting in a cheap shot at the replacement father: "A man owns the rooming house? Well it can't be very clean . . ." Joan picks up his violin case and he reacts aggressively. His mother tells him she would "really like" him to come home. "Mother just listen to me . . ." "Kenny, don't you talk to me in that tone of voice." Exasperated, he disconnects the call, which we see in a close-up shot of his hand holding what appears to be a piece of dark leather, bending it in his palm. I have always wondered: am I reading too much into it to think he's gripping it like the handle of a handgun? At this moment he's curving what he initially held as a flat object in his tense grip. Performing for Joan now, he continues to talk as if his mother is still on the line: "I love you too, mama, I really do." Then another cut to the Opry Belle where Barbara Jean is set to perform.

If simultaneity is the way *Nashville* builds its noisy, diffuse network, sequences like this one knap its buildup of unconscious drives to a finer (if still only partially exposed) point. Barbara Jean has been on her deathbed, in a sense, since the film's early stages. Kelly visits her in the hospital to pay respects and she's laid out like a corpse for a wake, illuminated by a lone lamplight, surrounded by get-well bouquets that look more like a wall of funereal flowers. What is it about Barbara Jean, we ask again and again without any clear answer on offer, that makes her so ill-suited to the world of Nashville in the 1970s, as if she were allergic to something in the air? Violence, sickness, decline, aging, and death are joked about, laughed at, dismissed, repressed, and tossed around freely throughout the film. The sheer number of guns or references to them seen and heard throughout creates a "metaphoric, infranarrative structure" that channels the energy of subliminal violence beneath direct awareness.[59] Haven chants American military heroism while Tom scoffs at Kelly's uniform as the garb of legalized murder; the majorettes twirl unloaded rifles while inside the airport terminal Joan stands next to a sign warning of weapon screenings; Lady Pearl carries openly while mourning Kennedy's death and recalling his spilled blood like it was a recurring nightmare; and all throughout the word "kill" is sublimated into showbiz speak, referring both to success and humiliating failure.

Even the screenplay, if you look at it closely while viewing, suggests a telling elision that pushes the causal dynamics flowing through the network further underground. At the Opry Belle, just after we have cut from Kenny in his room talking to his mother, Barnett is rebuffing Triplette's attempt to get Barbara Jean to headline the Walker rally ("No politics, no government, no nothin'," he says). Pvt. Kelly is up in front of the grandstand and Opal moseys on over; Kenny joins them after Barbara Jean's first song ends and seems to fall into a spell as he watches her perform "Dues," about the painful end of a relationship that has lost its loving warmth ("I want to be nice to you, treat you right / But how long can I pay these dues?"). In the middle of the song Opal leans over to Kelly with her microphone and asks, "Have you ever been to Vietnam?" "Was it awful?" Fixated on Barbara Jean, Kelly is nonplussed by Opal's questions. Then, according to Tewkesbury's screenplay, she asks, "Being a trained killer, do you carry a gun?" This line, however, is cut from the film. The next shot is of a troubled

Kenny looking over at them, as if in response to whatever was just said. With the excised bit of dialogue, it seems like he's responding to Kelly describing Vietnam as "hot and wet." If we imagine Opal's question back in, Kenny's glance takes on a different meaning. He then looks back toward the stage, but not at Barbara Jean. A matching Point-of-View (POV) shot captures Barnett, Triplette, and Delbert conversing in the wings, behind a column that splits them asymmetrically and creates a blind spot in Kenny's field of vision. Then back to Barbara Jean, and finally a reverse shot from behind her that reveals Kenny looking back at her from the front row, applauding. We can list the ellipses here: Opal's reference to guns and trained killing; the link between that question and Kenny's glance over at the political operatives (the men whose "dues" Barbara Jean continues to pay); the blind spot in Kenny's view of the three men; the movement of Kenny's look from the politicos back to Barbara Jean. The composition of the POV shot also links back to the earlier scene at The King of the Road, when Connie White takes the stage and momentarily dips out of sight behind a pole: "You can see me, I can't see you," she says, a line that is *not* in the screenplay.[60]

There is, we might say to all this, a motivational blind spot at *Nashville*'s core. And it is a blank emerging from two overlapping lacks: the lack of any protagonist-driven

FIGURE 13 *A backstage view.*

line elaborating need, desire, and aim (a gap inherent to network discourse); and the lack of reciprocity between what happens on stage and what happens off it (a gap in meaning grounding the storytelling discourses of popular song and political rhetoric). The more pressing blind spot, the invisible quilting point threading the entire network, is Walker himself, omnipresent only in his absence. Walker's role as one of Altman's clotheslines is not only to connect and progressively map the story world but to point at the same time to something unseeable within it, hidden like the man himself (or a copy of him, possibly just a recorded voice, like in *The Testament of Dr. Mabuse*) in his roving van. We can call the unseeable the subliminal, as Self does, in defense from who fault the film (and Altman's films generally) for including what appears to be an unmotivated climax, a random, meaningless eruption of violence toward an undeserving victim. I am suggesting, quite simply now, that those sorts of judgments attempt to translate *Nashville*'s network form back into narrative discourses that operate through direct, linear causality. Which is a symptom of the disturbing success of the final scene, generating a need to repress the suspected meaning of the movie's final collision. "Death," Self argues in an attempted paraphrase, "resides in the private relationships of these very public people, and death separates the lives of these insiders, the inventors and entertainers, from those outsiders who live with death, who recognize it, and who cause it."[61] Death *resides*, drifts like smoke, in and through the network—denied by the powerful (which may include some of the film's critics), gazed at by the powerless. We recall that Kenny goes to the rally directly from Mr. Green's wife's sparsely attended funeral, which they leave together in search of L. A. Joan.

If Kenny's shot seems to erupt from nowhere, unmotivated by any explicit or obvious goal, we should ask after the relationship between the climactic trigger pull and its oblique network of causes, the social distribution of guilt (as Opal already theorized, half-seriously). Which is not to say that Kenny's identity as shooter is irrelevant or epiphenomenal.

We have drawn a sketch of a story from the fragments of his appearances: his drifter's lifestyle, his mysterious violin case, his bumbling defense of Tommy Brown from the jibes of the irascible outsider Wade, his exasperated relationship to his mother, his piqued interest in the link between the backstage politico-managers and Barbara Jean. A quick summary of the assassination, then: Kenny moves forward and begins to unlock his violin case as Barbara Jean sings "My Idaho Home," a grateful, elegiac praise for loving, now-deceased parents and the romanticized home they shared. All the hints that someone is out to assassinate the rising populist Walker have somehow been transmuted in this moment as Barbara Jean either stands in for the "real" enemy—the more powerful public face of American values, real ideology in the frame of a well-meaning, fragile woman—or as a sacrificial lamb, or both. Cuts to Barbara Jean on stage in shallow focus occlude the Walker sign behind her: this is affective power, whatever you attribute it to, and the big American flag mutely billows to the music and maybe to an imagined but nonexistent (or not yet actualized, if we're optimistic) national community. With Haven on stage, more flowers in tow, Kenny takes his shot, and Barbara Jean falls, the screenplay describes, "like a beautiful bird shot in midflight." Pvt. Kelly attempts to apprehend the shooter, as Kenny is swallowed back into the crowd. Barnett rushes to his wife; Walker is gone. Haven, trying to take charge, describes the assault as an attack on "us," by "them."

The film does not set us up to agree inarguably with Haven's reaction, though. It is far too simple to draw a line like that, between all of us and all of them, though that's how it is usually done (I write this mere days after the assassination attempt on Donald Trump in Butler, Pennsylvania, and you can check the transcripts). Haven's crisis conscience suggests that all the anti-Americanism his career ostensibly served to root out from its hiding places—yet which he sees everywhere, even in a hippie's long hair—is condensed in Kenny's trigger finger. One might react against that idea by pointing to the assassin's idiosyncratic personal motivations (Hinckley did it for Jodie Foster, after all). Yet we do not have that either, with Kenny, only oblique hints about his personality. Can we understand his act as both intentional and as the climactic nexus of a sprawling, interpersonal network of psychic forces, social affects, and material differences? The more densely society is networked, the more glancing our knowledge of the many people at the peripheries of our lives, the more random intentional acts appear to us. Social life is a life of mindreading, and we try to do it even when we do not have the means for it—not just with mutual friends or acquaintances but with mass shooters, terrorists, and true crime anti-heroes.

With Kenny, it might not be just, as many critics have suggested, that he realizes after his time wandering Nashville that the culture industry is now more powerful than our elected officials. The best we can do, in this case, is conjecture: Kenny is the kind of person who has long idealized popular music as an escape from the dreary experience of the American family he has lived, but he's been progressively disillusioned by the people who actually run the show (hence his glance between Barbara Jean and the men in the wings at the Belle). We might imagine, in a common and reasonable reading, that he was always intending to assassinate Walker, but that he turned his gun on Barbara Jean when he realized they were ultimately two

FIGURE 14 *Barbara Jean, icon.*

sides of the same coin, two voices of an underlying American sickness. Or maybe his choice was a bit different: on a meta-characterological level, we might imagine that Kenny was either going to pull a fiddle or a gun out of his case by the end of the film, he was either going to be a lone wolf assassin or the new member of an upstart country music band, and the decider was the town of Nashville itself. Kenny's final decision is made in full witness of the falseness he comes to believe Barbara Jean embodies as a female star, as the sincere messenger from an untruthful past, an "Idaho Home" belied not only by his domineering mother but by all the men he sees propping up the illusion for their own benefit, and by the near-vacant funeral service for an invisible woman (Mr. Green's wife) who lay on her deathbed while her own niece was out chasing celebrities around town. That Barbara Jean transports Kenny emotionally is precisely why her siren song must be snuffed out.

That all makes Kenny seem the avenging angel, and that is right, but he is also just an ordinary dude, the kind of person who comes to town (like so many others, like Albuquerque, who gets the last word in the film, and I will give it to her too in a second) and is turned one way or another by the interactions that shape his open future. When the beauty of the ideal—of family, motherhood, nation, music—reveals itself to be a pile of pop images all the way down, a bullet might seem to be the only thing that can pierce the veil, that can break through and touch the real that surely must still be there behind the fragile, pasteboard martyr they keep sending up against her own best interests. If this is the best route for Kenny to express himself publicly, to exercise his wounded masculinity, or just to be *somebody* amidst the mass of nobodies he emerges from, that speaks as much about the limitations and inequalities of the world of Nashville/*Nashville*—of the network as a web of indirect schemes, aggressions, misreadings, and misunderstandings—as it does about him as a person, or as a character. If that was an uncomfortable proposition for an audience gearing up for America's bicentennial to entertain, imagine how they felt watching the rest of the century unfold.

It Don't Worry Me (or, Everything Is Disconnected)

A long time before network cinema promised the pleasure and relief of finding how everyone and everything is connected—balm for the lonely anomie of late modernity—ancient Greek tragedy promised a similar sort of realization through the presence of its cities' gods and seers and their guiding (if not always beneficent) hands. In Aristotle's unparalleled history and poetics of tragedy, with Sophocles' *Oedipus Rex* at its apex, unities of space, time, and action make for superbly coherent plots in which all individual parts are swept up into a single whole at a moment of belated recognition. Everything is connected (so Oedipus shockingly discovers), but formally we could not be further away from the messy sprawl of network narratives, especially those in which sheer unmotivated accident joins otherwise far-flung characters. As we have seen, however, the broader a narrative's network the more work its discourse must do to achieve some minimal coherence, thematically or plotwise. Many network films take great pains to gather all their moving parts up, in the end, and demonstrate the interconnectivity that finally justifies their otherwise tenuous coexistence in the discourse. A climactic wedding party, say, where everyone connects through their love of the bride, or in an airport terminal waiting to board a doomed flight. In the happier moments, we sense the triumph of collectivity redeeming prior melancholic feelings of isolation. In the sadder ones, we feel at least that we share our miserable fate with other people.

Nashville's final scene is one of a few big hubs in the film—airport, traffic jam, concert, public rally—but it does not do everything we might wish it would. Barbara Jean's assassination is cathartic, perhaps, in that it releases an aggressive tension that had crisscrossed the network from the film's opening minutes. And its storylines, abbreviated and fragmentary as they are, appear to intersect at this very moment, with most of the main ensemble witness to and directly impacted by the violent act. But if we imagine that Kenny's shocking, heinous deed will bring everyone together, the stars and the wannabes and the cynics and the working folks, we are initially disappointed. Everyone seems to scatter in the chaos: Haven addresses the crowd; Barnett struggles to stop the bleeding; Walker's limousine flees the scene with his police escort; Delbert leads a wounded Haven offstage; Kelly numbly walks back out through the crowd; Triplette slowly drifts into damage control; Tom, Tommy, and Bud jump in to lend a hand with Barbara Jean; Sueleen stands mute off the side, her dream squashed; Lady Pearl stays in her seat, as if she's seen this all before; Linnea, frozen, unsure of where to go or what to do, is pulled offstage by Delbert; Opal wanders through the crowd, asking everyone what she missed when she was in the truck; Albuquerque, microphone thrust into her hand, starts to sing. Everyone and everything is disconnected, tossed to the wind, because the event means something different to everyone. "This isn't Dallas, this is Nashville," Haven exhorts, and he is too right. The national fabric he has hoped to repair by the force of his charisma—Make America Wholesome Again—has already unraveled. Everyone there on stage is joined by absence, by conflict. And not just by a lack at the center of American identity. They are also magnetized by the paradoxical, fictional mediator that forms everyone into an audience of lonely individuals, connected through disconnection: the commodity, the recording, the poster image, the record we were sold at the very beginning of the film, which is also the movie we have been watching. Everything in *Nashville* is production, consumption, and reproduction. America too is being pitched for a new episode in its ongoing series of adventures.

And yet: we end on a most moving spectacle. Remember Albuquerque, who has never gotten her shot to show us what she's made of, until now. She is in the right place at the right time, despite all the tragedy, because she has been all over the place, just hanging on. Her triumph, we might admit, is possible only through the network, as a statistical law of large numbers of chances. Indeed, she breaks into *Nashville*'s now-classic standby, "It Don't Worry Me." Replacing not only Barbara Jean and Tom but Linnea too, Albuquerque sings with the backing of the Black gospel choir, the closest thing we have here to a Greek chorus. As their song builds, we see shots of faces singing along in the crowd—men, women, children. What do we make of this ritual, beautiful as it is, following so quickly on Barbara Jean's demise? "Life may be a one-way street," Albuquerque sings, "But it don't worry me." *Nashville* is hardly a one-way street, all zigzags and roundabouts and cross-track sound. Still, despite the appearance of such freedom of movement, what does it all amount to? Which club to spend one's evening and paycheck at; which record to buy; which guy or gal to pick up at the bar; Republican or Democrat (or, maybe, Independent); Miller or Bud; a hot dog or a hamburger. The beauty of song is that we can finally all sing together—liberal or conservative, man or woman, Black or white—but we also wonder in this moment, as every other character makes their own way out, desires and dreams crushed or put on hold, whether music really makes nothing else happen beyond its moment of transport. Same with movies, we fear. Or we will after the credits roll. For another minute or two, it don't worry us one bit.

Notes

1 David Thomson, *The Whole Equation: A History of Hollywood* (New York: Little, Brown, 2005), 183.
2 Ibid., 184.
3 For a thorough account of the film's production, see Jan Stuart, *The Nashville Chronicles: The Making of Robert Altman's Masterpiece* (New York: Simon & Schuster, 2000).
4 Joan Tewkesbury, "Dialogue on Film," *American Film* (March 1979), 43.
5 Mitchell Zuckoff, *Robert Altman: The Oral Biography* (New York: Knopf, 2009), 275.

6 The caricatures on the album cover were drawn by J. William Myers, a local Nashville artist working around the shoot with freelancer Harry Haun. Bert Remsen (who played Star in the film), saw Myers's illustrations on the last day of shooting and brought him to show Altman, who reportedly responded, "When in hell did you do this? You've captured my movie." See Stuart, 279.
7 Robert Niemi, *The Cinema of Robert Altman: Hollywood Maverick* (New York: Wallflower Press, 2016), 78.
8 Frank Caso, *Robert Altman: In the American Grain* (London: Reaktion Books, 2015), 113.
9 David Bordwell, *Poetics of Cinema* (New York: Routledge, 2008), 114.
10 Mark Minett thoroughly rejects the "antinarrative" claim, for instance, arguing that

> Altman's strategy [throughout his career] was built on a foundation of classical Hollywood narrative structure. . . . Altman's films synthesize classical structuring strategies with a suite of narrational approaches that are elaborative perversions of classicism. These approaches couple many of the key techniques and affordances of classical narration with nonclassical principles in the service of goals that invert or redirect their conventional purposes.

See Minett, *Robert Altman and the Elaboration of Hollywood Storytelling* (New York: Oxford University Press, 2021), 27.
11 Greil Marcus, "On E. L. Doctorow's *Ragtime* and Robert Altman's *Nashville*," in Greil Marcus, *The Dustbin of History* (Cambridge, MA: Harvard University Press, 1997), 91, 93–4.
12 Kristin Thompson, *Storytelling in the New Hollywood: Understanding Classical Narrative Technique* (Cambridge, MA: Harvard University Press, 1999), 12.
13 Stuart, 60.
14 Ibid., 72–3.
15 Bordwell, 198.
16 Robin Wood, "Smart-Ass and Cutie-Pie: Notes toward an Evaluation of Robert Altman," *Movie* 21 (1975): 2.
17 Robert T. Self, *Robert Altman's Subliminal Reality* (Minneapolis: University of Minnesota Press, 2002), 3.
18 Ibid., 4.

19 Dora Zhang, "Notes on Atmosphere," *Qui Parle* 27.1 (2018): 130.
20 David Bordwell names Altman's *M*A*S*H* (1970) as one of the films that "elaborated" this technique:

> From a wide-angle view of the setting the filmmaker might zoom in and pan with the actors as they played out the scene; still tighter zooms would be reserved for moments of crucial drama. This "searching and revealing" approach, allowing the camera to scan the action and overtly pick out key details, became a significant norm of the 1960s and 1970s.

On the History of Film Style, 2nd ed. (Madison: Irvington Way Press, 2018), 249.
21 See John Belton and Lyle Tector, "The Bionic Eye: The Aesthetics of the Zoom," *Film Comment* 16.5 (1980): 13.
22 Minett, 80.
23 Belton and Tector, 14.
24 Richard T. Jameson, "Writin' it Down Kinda Makes Me Feel Better': Robert Altman's *Nashville*," *Movietone News* 43 (1975).
25 Minett, 98.
26 Aaron Kunin, *Character as Form* (London: Bloomsbury, 2019), 73.
27 Meir Sternberg, *Expositional Modes and Temporal Ordering in Fiction* (Bloomington: Indiana University Press, 1978), 26.
28 Ibid., 53.
29 Alex Woloch, *The One vs. the Many: Minor Characters and the Space of the Protagonist in the Novel* (Princeton: Princeton University Press, 2003), 30–1.
30 Ibid., 31.
31 Ibid., 58–9.
32 Bordwell, 204.
33 Evan Smith, "Thread Structure: Rewriting the Hollywood Formula," *Journal of Film and Video* 51.3–4 (Fall/Winter 1999/2000): 90.
34 Robert Altman and David Thomson, *Altman on Altman* (New York: Faber and Faber, 2005), 164–5, italics mine.
35 See Stuart, 210.
36 Bordwell, 196.
37 Stuart, 145.
38 Ibid., 65.

39 Niemi, 78.
40 Stuart, 217.
41 Though perhaps not in every way. Unlike *Nashville* (or really unlike almost every other film), *California Split* contains no non-/extra-diegetic sound. All sound or music that appears to function that way is soon revealed to have a specific locus in the story world. As Philip Brophy recognizes, "aural realism" is the textural function co-amplified by the wholly diegetic soundtrack and the radical immanence of the soundscape, which blends plot-motivated dialogue between principal characters William (Bill) and Charlie with everything else that makes noise around them. Far less of a network film than *Nashville*, however, *California Split*'s soundtrack is tuned more closely to traditional patterns of plot and character development: "When there is an excess of sound (the horse track, card games and poker halls) the narrative conveys a continuum of character action. When there is noticeable silence (as in William's many reflective moments) the narrative signals a change in character orientation." See Brophy, *100 Modern Soundtracks* (London: British Film Institute, 2004), 51. As much as the film dissolves speech into din and protagonist motivation into a network of ongoing human and non-human activity, a more encompassing soundtrack pattern re-structures and re-psychologizes sound.
42 Rick Altman, "24-Track Narrative? Robert Altman's *Nashville*," *Cinémas* 1.3 (1991): 104.
43 Sid Levin, "The Art of the Editor: *Nashville*," *Filmmakers Newsletter* 8.10 (1975).
44 Altman, "24-Track Narrative," 113.
45 Joan Tewkesbury, *Nashville: An Original Screenplay* (New York: Bantam Books, 1976), n.p.
46 Jacques Rancière, *The Politics of Aesthetics* (London: Bloomsbury, 2013), 12.
47 Stuart, 191.
48 Pauline Kael, "Robert Altman's Funny, Epic Vision of America," *The New Yorker* (March 3, 1975), 79.
49 See Gayle Sherwood Magee, *Robert Altman's Soundtracks: Film, Music, and Sound from* M*A*S*H *to* A Prairie Home Companion (Oxford: Oxford University Press, 2014), chapter 4.
50 Rick Altman, *The American Film Musical* (Bloomington: Indiana University Press, 1988), 273.

51 Billy Sherill: "I'll tell you what I liked best about the film—when they shot that miserable excuse for a country-music singer." Minnie Pearl: "I'm afraid a lot of people who love our music will be offended by the film. The music was terrible." Jeannie Pruett: "Those songs never would've made it out of Nashville. I'd be hard pressed to name the one I hated the most." Lynn Anderson: "I was *personally* affronted by the music. They didn't make it clear that it was tongue-in-cheek. . . . The part I hate the most is that the uninitiated will think all of us must be bad or that all of us create that horrible music they had. I hope to God *my* music doesn't sound like that!" Lloyd Green: "I thought the music was atrocious." These are only some of the angry, negative reactions from Nashville musicians and lifers collected by Stuart. See Stuart, 292–3.
52 Altman, *American Film Musical*, 326.
53 Helene Keyssar, *Robert Altman's America* (New York: Oxford University Press, 1991), 162.
54 Ibid., 164.
55 Richard R. Ness, "'Doing Some Replacin': Gender, Genre and the Subversion of Dominant Ideology in the Music Scores," in *Robert Altman: Critical Essays*, ed. Rick Armstrong (Jefferson: McFarland, 2011), 49–50.
56 Stuart, 63.
57 Ibid., 140–1.
58 See, for instance, Bruce Robbins, *The Servant's Hand: English Fiction from Below* (Durham: Duke University Press, 1993).
59 Self, 193.
60 See Juli Kearns's Internet essay, "The Mysteries of Robert Altman's *Nashville*," the only source I have found that tracks these parallels in depth (https://idyllopuspress.com/idyllopus/film/nashville.htm).
61 Self, 195.

CONCLUSION

Why study, critique, write about, and—most importantly—teach network films today? And why do all those things with theory not only in mind, but front and center? Arguably the biggest challenge in teaching a film like *Nashville* is its imposing runtime, which is not even atypical for network films (just as network novels, historically, tend toward the multi-volume and large-cast television series or soaps can run forever). Many people cannot imagine drawing charts or mapping character systems while viewing a movie, and most of us do not have even the rudimentary coding skills to do so efficiently. Is network cinema a phenomenon doomed to be enjoyed (or not) but ultimately consigned to an academic and pedagogical niche, the province of a few foolhardy souls? And is network theory just a sprawling interdisciplinary collection of resources that may be helpful when taken piecemeal but is too loose a field to ever govern, say, undergraduate courses in cinema studies? It would be overconfident of me to answer those last two questions with definitive noes. But in closing, I can at least give my best, briefest answer to the first two, and then let the future take its course.

Maybe networks are so unavoidable that to ignore their representations, to not pursue investigations of network forms, would mean forgoing critical consideration of a fundamental part of our culture. Or one of its fantasmatic supports. "A new 'life experience' is in the air," Slavoj Žižek writes, "a perception of life that explodes the form of the linear, centered narrative and renders life as a multiform flow."[1] If we are now more than ever "haunted by the chanciness of life and the alternate versions of reality," network cinema and its variations may be the ultimate fantasy projection of our collective ghost existence.

Žižek mentions Altman's *Short Cuts* (contingent encounters, meaningless intersections) and Krzysztof Kieslowski's *Blind Chance*, *The Double Life of Veronique*, and *Red* (alternative possible worlds, parallel existences). Something about contemporary life generates either perceptions or fantasies of reality as "one of the possible—often even not the most probable—outcomes of an 'open' situation, this notion that other possible outcomes are not simply canceled out but continue to haunt our 'true' reality as a specter of what might have happened, conferring on our reality the status of extreme fragility and contingency."[2] Granted, the haunting of the living by unlived lives has informed literature for centuries. Aeneas meets Dido's shade in the underworld and sheds tears of pity, if not complete regret, for his lover's tragic end (and, in a belated recognition, his heroic drive's role in it). Could things have been otherwise? Maybe not, if the epic's circular *telos* mitigates a large amount of narrative chance.

Žižek's point is that if we experience reality as multiple rather than singular, which he believes we do now, then narrative creation will no longer designate "the positive act of imposing a new order, but rather the negative gesture of choice, of limiting the possibilities, of privileging one option at the expense of others," which ultimately demands narrative forms capable (1) of *expressing* the fragile multiplicity of contemporary life governed by anxieties of choice, and (2) *foregrounding* the multiplicity of possible links closed by each individual story path.[3] Network films like Altman's or alternative world films like Kieslowski's are preparatory works on the path toward cyberspace hypertexts, in which our new condition finds its "appropriate objective correlative." This "new experience of the world," I have suggested throughout this book, is overdetermined by a good number of causes, though *neoliberalism* is often used to collect many of them in one historical concept. Fredric Jameson captures its advent, the moment of the emergence of the multinational network, as "a new and historically original dilemma, one that involves our insertion as individual subjects into a multidimensional set of radically discontinuous realities, whose frames range from the still surviving spaces of bourgeois private life all the way to the unimaginable decentering of global capital itself."[4] What Jameson calls *cognitive mapping*, as we have discussed, is a symptomatic expression of multinational, networked capitalism, an aesthetic response to the subject's confused place in the abstract, unrepresentable global totality. We can easily hypothesize that the emergence of network films like *Nashville* in the 1970s—a convenient but reasonable decade to mark in the history of neoliberalism, with the 1971 end of the Bretton Woods system of fixed exchange rates—along with other system-mapping genres like the conspiracy film, expressed a desire (or felt need) to corral a vastly complexifying totality with newly expanded narrative forms. And it is no coincidence, we might continue, that network cinema mushroomed in the Clintonian 1990s, along with post-Soviet end-of-history feel-good liberalism, the dot com boom, and the parade of Third Way market deregulations leading to the 1999 repeal of Glass-Steagall.

If network form is an attempt to mediate the ostensibly unmappable totalities that exceed the individual in every direction, then network cinema on its own has much to teach us about the role narrative plays in accommodating history (economic, political, technological, art-cultural) as it evolves and develops new contradictions. New network cinemas—hyperlink, user-participatory, online—present another stage in the process of cognitively mapping historical and epistemic conditions through audiovisual form. And if network theory, at this point, is less of a sturdy body of literature than a loosely sewn mesh of intellectual links across disciplines (philosophy, mathematics, sociology, media history, literary and film criticism just to start), we ought to consider the project of articulating a more coherent corpus—a project this book hopefully contributes to in a small, modest, though far from complete way—as part of the same general program as the formation of network narratives. At their best, network theory and narrative, with network cinema at the forefront, together connect (piecemeal rather than all at once) otherwise distinct phenomena without ignoring or simply affirming as necessary or natural the social forces that shape networks in particular, non-random ways. Social, industrial, and commercial networks are wholes that follow tendencies in their codes, in the virtual logic by which links are formed and reinforced (whether that logic derives from biological facts, principles of capital accumulation, digital protocols or sorting algorithms, or the vicissitudes of human desire). Network theory is all about uncovering those tendencies that magnetize the webs we travel in, communicate by, and are channeled through. Network film embodies them, makes them available for provisional perception, through expanded character systems, oblique plotting, narratorial omniscience, circulatory motifs, and thematic or structural unities built in tension with all its centrifugal energies.

Altman's *Nashville* is, by design, a noisy, messy network. Is it the right text to use to exemplify the affordances, limitations, and pleasures of network thinking? There is no perfectly representative network film, just as there is no single network topology, and that is a good thing. At the same time, without integrating formalism with network theory, we risk courting the most opportunistic—sometimes even pernicious—uses of network terminology, celebrating flexibility, decentralization, multiplicity, and randomness regardless of the ideological roles they might serve under late capitalist regimes. *Nashville*'s network configuration is ideologically ambivalent, even contradictory, which makes it worth watching closely and thinking deeply about. It reveals, on the one hand, the subtleties of power and inequality as they flow through networks rather than explicit hierarchies and centralized structures. It also offers the joyous pleasures of connecting, mapping, and socializing—activities that intimate an unrealized democratic world beyond the horizon of our damaged present. The networked world *Nashville* represents is riven with disconnection, loneliness, and exploitation. Through it also shine promises of human attachment, the delicious magnetism of humor, and a broader capacity for visibility across social divides. *Nashville* is about the true *and* false promises of network form. "If we don't live peaceful," Albuquerque warns in the film's last bit of unsolicited advice, "there's gonna be nothin' left in our graves except Clorox bottles and plastic fly swatters with red dots on 'em."

Notes

1 Slavoj Žižek, *Enjoy Your Symptom!* (New York: Routledge Classics, 2008), 233.
2 Ibid., 234.
3 Ibid.
4 Fredric Jameson, *Postmodernism, or, The Cultural Logic of Late Capitalism* (Durham: Duke University Press, 1991), 413.

FURTHER READING

Albert-László Barabási, *Linked: The New Science of Networks* (Cambridge: Perseus, 2002).
   An accessible introduction to network science, the first written for a popular audience, by the physicist whose work challenged prevailing ideas about randomness in networks.

David Bordwell, *Poetics of Cinema* (New York: Routledge, 2008).
   One of many books to consult by the film narratologist most responsible for our capacity to understand how network forms work in the movies, a topic sprinkled throughout his corpus. See in particular the chapter titled, "Mutual Friends and Chronologies of Chance."

David Bordwell, *The Way Hollywood Tells It: Story and Style in Modern Movies* (Berkeley: University of California Press, 2006).
   More specifically about the continuities of mass-market Hollywood filmmaking into the post-classical age, Bordwell discusses the historical flexibility of network films in the chapter, "Subjective Stories and Network Narratives."

Mark Buchanan, *Nexus: Small Worlds and the Groundbreaking Science of Networks* (New York: Norton, 2002).
   Another accessible work on broad applications of network theory, especially small-worlds models.

Manuel Castells, *The Rise of the Network Society*, 2nd ed. (Chichester: Wiley-Blackwell, 2010).
   A field-defining book on the globalization of network society and the socio-economic dynamics of the so-called information age.

Alexander R. Galloway and Eugene Thacker, *The Exploit: A Theory of Networks* (Minneapolis: University of Minnesota Press, 2013).

A case for the invasiveness of the network form in contemporary life and culture, against the idea of networks as inherently egalitarian, and for a new definition of control native to networks.

Alexander R. Galloway, *Protocol: How Control Exists after Decentralization* (Cambridge, MA: MIT Press, 2006).

A foundational exploration of the protocols that guide distributed networks, charting the forms control takes after economic and informational decentralization.

Patrick Jagoda. *Network Aesthetics* (Chicago: University of Chicago Press, 2016).

Now the primary source on popular culture's mediation of affects and experiences symptomatic of networked life and society, and art and media's role in constructing and managing interconnection. The author considers both traditional network narratives and interactive digital media.

Bruno Latour, *Reassembling the Social: An Introduction to Actor-Network-Theory* (Oxford: Oxford University Press, 2005).

One of several relevant books by the philosopher-sociologist at the center of Actor-Network Theory, this is one of the best sources for understanding how ANT reconceptualizes the "social" as an active, ongoing assemblage of relations.

Caroline Levine, *Forms: Whole, Rhythm, Hierarchy, Network* (Princeton: Princeton University Press, 2017).

A case for critical formalism as a means for bridging aesthetic, cultural, and political knowledge, Levine includes networks as one of four major ordering forms (discussing *The Wire* as a primary example).

Gayle Sherwood Magee, *Robert Altman's Soundtracks: Film, Music, and Sound from* M*A*S*H *to* A Prairie Home Companion (Oxford: Oxford University Press, 2014).

Among the many useful books on Altman as a filmmaker, this is the most extensive study of his use of music and sound.

Mark Minett, *Robert Altman and the Elaboration of Hollywood Storytelling* (New York: Oxford University Press, 2021).
   My vote for the best book on Altman so far. Demystifies some of the major assumptions about his style while establishing Altman as a pragmatic innovator in cinematic storytelling.

Anna Munster, *An Aesthesia of Networks: Conjunctive Experience in Art and Technology* (Cambridge, MA: MIT Press, 2013).
   A study of how networks experience, the operations they perform, and the changes they produce. Focuses on a wide range of contemporary artistic and cultural practices that engage network technologies and techniques.

Steven Shaviro, *Connected, or What It Means to Live in the Network Society* (Minneapolis: University of Minnesota Press, 2003).
   An aphoristic, highly speculative guide to cyberculture and the network society that keeps its ear to the ground. Shaviro emphasizes science fiction in its many medial forms.

Alex Woloch, *The One vs. the Many: Minor Characters and the Space of the Protagonist in the Novel* (Princeton: Princeton University Press, 2003).
   A magisterial study of character in literature that introduces the idea of character-spaces and character-systems that structure the discourse of the novel. Offers a compelling analytical model for understanding how character networks work to construct the dynamic worlds of any narrative text.

INDEX

11:14 (2003) 85–7, 90

actor-network theory
  (ANT) 64, 67–8, 72, 74
aestheticized networks 77
Altman, Rick 151, 155, 158
Altman, Robert 1, 103, 107
  anti-classical
    filmmaking 122
  "centrality" to American
    cinema 121
  characters 143, 145
  classical Hollywood
    plotting 122
  filmmaking of 116
  films 129, 131
  Nashville (*see* Nashville)
  recording system 150
  Short Cuts 140–1, 194
  soundtracks 155
  subliminal zooms 123
American individualism
  111
American music/Black
  music 146
Atlas of the European Novel
  (Moretti) 31
atmosphere 122

Babel (2006) 45–6
Barabási, Albert-László 54–6
Bleak House (Dickens) 30

body microphones 153
Bordwell, David 10, 12, 20, 92, 114, 121
Borges, Jorge Luis 80–1
Bretton Woods system 195
Brown, Bill 73
The Butterfly Effect
  (2004) 87, 89

California Split (1974) 150
Calvinoesque fantasy 30
Castells, Manuel 36
Chaplin, Geraldine 145
character network 57, 113, 131, 144, 169, 175
character space 62, 127
character transparency 115
Chun, Wendy Hui Kyong 38–40
Citizens Band (CB) radio 60
classical Hollywood
  cinema 23, 115, 117, 151
cognitive mapping 35, 45, 76, 195
coincidences 85–6
Comédie Humaine
  (Balzac) 31
complex whole concept 65
conceptual artworks 74
*Connected, or What It Means
  to Live in the Network
  Society* (Shaviro) 3

consciousness 26
    collective 28
    individual 26, 28
    individual *vs.* collective 27
    Jamesian stream of 77
    self-consciousness 125
control societies 37–8
Coover, Robert 82
country music 103–4, 146
Crash (2004) 7
cybernetics 39

data visualization
    programs 77
decentralized network
    society 37
Deleuze, Gilles 37
diachronic blindness 50–1
Dickens, Charles 30, 32
digital cartography 82
digital gaming 79
digital mosaics 83
disciplinary societies 37–8
Discipline and Punish
    (Foucault) 37
Durkheim, Émile 25–6,
    28
Durkheimian sociology 25

Emma (Austen) 128
English Traits (Emerson) 5
Equal Credit Opportunity
    Act 166
Erdős-Rényi model 54, 56
Euler, Leonhard 17
Eulerian path 18
Everything is Different
    (*Ötvenkét vasárnap*)
    (Karinthy) 18
existential exorcism 64

finance capitalism 35
Foucault, Michel 37

Galloway, Alexander R. 29,
    37, 50, 52
global village network
    ideology 45
Goo Goo Cluster 162–5
Google 53
Grand Hotel (1932) 13, 90
Granovetter, Mark 42
graph theory 18, 25, 50, 52
Griffith, D. W. 104

Habermasian utopia 36
Hamlet (Shakespeare) 56,
    59–60
Handle with Care (Citizens
    Band, 1977) 60–2
Harman, Graham 63, 69,
    73
Harvey, David 41
Hiltz, Starr Roxanne 36
A History of Greece
    (Thirlwall) 5
Hollywood scripts 104
Hollywood's Golden Age
    104
Honky Tonk Freeway
    (1981) 13
Howards End (Schlegel) 2
hyper-connected society 20

I Heart Huckabees (2004) 7
The Image of the City
    (Lynch) 45
imagination 26
Iñárritu, Alejandro
    González 45
Internet 12, 40

Jagoda, Patrick 3, 11, 35, 79
James, Henry 41, 90
James, William 77
Jameson, Fredric 34, 44, 194–5

kaleidoscopic mosaics 82
Karinthy, Frigyes 18
kinship networks 30
Kochen, Manfred 48

late capitalism 41, 44
Latour, Bruno 63, 65, 71, 74
Leibniz, Gottfried Wilhelm 62
Levine, Caroline 29, 33
liberal pluralism 63
liberal social theory 25
Lions Gate 8-Track Sound System 150
Little Dorrit (Bleak House) 30
Local Area Network (LAN) 30
Lombardi, Mark 74, 76
Lukács, Georg 42

mana 66
Marcus, Greil 117
Mass Ornament 78
Mazzarella, William 66
Milgram, Stanley 47
modern anthropology 66
Moretti, Franco 57
Moretti's Hamlet network 58–9
Mosaic (2017) 78–9
mosaics 83
Moulthrop, Stuart 81
multi-protagonist films 23
multiverse 81

Nashville 2, 95, 103, 116, 193; *see also* network theory
24-track recording 150–3
asymmetric character systems 130
atmosphere 123
audiovisual relationships 120, 126
Barbara Jean (character) 125, 128–9, 164, 176, 179–80, 182, 184, 186
character groupings 113
character network 108, 141–3
character pairs 111–12
churches characters 114
cinematography 123–4
clotheslines 118
Connie White (character) 113, 142–3
everything is connected 185
exceptional scenes 167
exposition of 128–9
female characters of 165–7
final scene 175–85
Goo Goo Cluster 161–5
Hal Phillip Walker's vision for America 106
Kenny Frasier (charcter) 172–4, 180, 182, 184
L. A. Joan (character) 132
Lady Pearl (character) 166, 179, 186
Linnea Reese (character) 113, 159, 170

main players 109–11
Mary (character) 158
minor characters 171
Mr. Green (character) 129, 132, 176–7
narrative structure 117, 126–8
network configuration 196
nodes of network 139
Norman (character) 125, 169
Opal (character) 145–9
opening credits 107–8
recording studio 152
screenplay 151, 180
social realism 155
song 154–61
sonic networks 153
soundtracks 153
static network graph 144
Sueleen Gay (character) 158, 160, 170, 186
supernumeraries 169–70
thread structures 140–1
Tom Frank (character) 156, 158, 179
traffic jam 133–7
Tricycle Man (character) 124–5
Nashville (city) 103
circles within circles 105
music culture 105
Tewkesbury's trip 105
neoliberal capitalism 44
neoliberalism 35, 194–5
network 5
cities 31
in cultural studies 29

Eulerian path 51
"everything is connected" 3, 7
global network of 36
graphing narratives 56
kinship networks 30
Latour's account of 69
literature forms 33
modern graph theory 49
narrative art 42
resilience of 49
socioeconomic history 35
sociology of 26
topologies of 52
translations 70–1
transportation 30
visual form 35
vs. systems 70
weak connectivity 49
Network Aesthetics (Jagoda) 3, 34
network cinema 11
audiovisual form 195
cultural influence 11
early 1990s 10
network narratives 10
new marketing models 11
postmodern pastiche 11
thread structure 21
network films 21, 88–9, 91, 119, 196
network maps 31
network narratives 23, 43, 174
connections between characters 86
narrative forms 22
non-linear feedback loops 87
and non-network narratives 60

omniscience effects 94
protagonist-driven forms 94
shared-time principle 92
social infrastructures 93
Network Nation (Hiltz) 36
network theory 1, 195–6
aestheticized networks 77
coincidences 85
conceptual artworks 74–5
connectivity 2
diversity of 4
everything is connected 8
graphing networks 47–52
graphing of 56–62
narrative forms 195
and *Nashville* 14–15 (see also Nashville)
and network cinema 10–14
omniscience 90–4
participatory vs. non-participatory narratives 79
of society 29
theoretical pluralism 63
web 53–5
New Hollywood cinema 2
New network cinemas 195

open architecture 39
Our Mutual Friend (Dickens) 30–1

PageRank algorithm 53
The Pasteurization of France (Latour) 63
The Pickwick Papers (Dickens) 30
plot resolution 21
Point-of-View (POV) shots 79
Pool, Ithiel de Sola 48

Postscript on Control Societies (Deleuze) 37
The Prince and the Pauper (Twain) 73
protagonist 23, 61
Pulp Fiction 22, 33, 172–5

radical empiricism 77
Rapoport, Anatol 49
residual spiritualism 66
resonance 121
Roderick Hudson (James) 41
Rudolph, Alan 141, 168
The Rules of the Sociological Method (Durkheim) 25

scale-free networks 54–5
Seinfeld (1989–98) 33–4
self-consciousness 84, 125, 128, 156
Seven Bridges of Königsberg 17, 51
Shakespearean characters 56
Shannon, Claude 39
Shaviro, Steven 40
Shaviro's network society model 40
The Simpsons (1989–present) 33
Six Degrees of Kevin Bacon 19
small-world experiments 48
Smith, Adam 25
Smith, Evan 21
social facts 25
Durkheim's analysis of 28
social laws 28
suicide 28
social network theory 25
Solomonoff, Ray 49

space-time compression   131
static network graphs   139
Storyspace   82
The Strength of Weak Ties
      (Granovetter)   42
subliminal reality   122
Suicide (Durkheim)   27
sympathy   26
Syriana (2005)   44, 46–7
systems theory   52, 55

A Tale of Two Cities
      (Dickens)   32
Tewkesbury, Joan   103, 105,
      117, 151, 157, 165
Thacker, Eugene   29, 50, 52
theory of (cyber-)network
      society   40
Thieves Like Us (1974)   157
thingification   73
thing theory   73
Thompson, Kristin   22
titular societies   37
traditional mosaics   83
Turoff, Murray   36
Twain, Mark   73

ubiquitous computing   40
US legal history   130
utilitarian social theories   25

Victory Garden
      (Moulthrop)   81, 83
virtual financial markets   36
virtual worlds   40

War and Peace (Tolstoy)   31
Watts, Duncan J.   42
web   53–5
Webb, Jim   144, 150
Wedge   40
We Have Never Been Modern
      (Latour)   70
*What's Wrong With This
      Picture?* (*Tid til
      Forandring*) (2004)   21
Wiener, Norbert   38
The Wire (2002–8)   33
Wood, Robin   121
World Wide Web   55, 58

Zhang, Dora   122
Žižek, Slavoj   193–4